art
for today's schools

DAVIS PUBLICATIONS, Inc.
Worcester, Massachusetts

GEORGE F. HORN, Supervisor of Art
Baltimore City Public Schools, Maryland

Copyright 1967
DAVIS PUBLICATIONS, INC.
Worcester, Massachusetts
Library of Congress Catalog Card Number: 67-17976
SBN 87192–001–8
Second Printing, 1969
Teachers' Reference Edition
Graphic Design by the Author

CONTENTS

Knowledge of art evolves out of not one but several ways of learning, each concurrent and equally contributing. There is the making of art, the personal involvement in the creative process. Through a critical dialogue about art, meanings and possibilities are explored. A study of the history of art reveals the impact it has had on the spirit of man and the way he has used it to express his hopes and frustrations. Books such as this one are designed to stimulate inquiry and nurture a continuous and critical dialogue about art and its meaning for you.

The author has sought to help his readers become aware of the many forms art takes.

There are different means for experiencing art—involvement, criticism, and a study of our art heritage as mentioned above. But there are ways beyond this. Dean Trottenberger of Harvard University suggests that we need to be conscious of art as it is manifested outside the studio and museum walls; urban planning, conservation, communication media and other everyday visual aspects surround us. He suggests through experiencing art we may become visually literate. The value in this book lies not in its immediate impact on you but its lingering effects in making you visually literate. It should be a threshold for continuous quest of art in the life before you. The art of the past and present is no predictor of the art yet to come. However, through learning about it one thing comes through clearly—great art has a common denominator of aesthetic quality, universal and timeless.

We are challenged to become involved in and with art as a continuously evolving experience meaningful now and tomorrow.

Dr. Ivan E. Johnson
Florida State University

What can one expect of a book dealing with the arts and designed for teachers? Certainly a rich visual form is essential, possessing exciting layout and an abundance of fine and appropriate photographs. While mention of the art accomplishments of the past should be apparent, for cultural heritage must not be denied, the major emphasis should be directed towards the language and structure of contemporary art. And a plea for the future appears appropriate. Proper suggestions for student involvement are also a need. The range should be comprehensive, yet with helpful specifics. Thus an effective blending of art, past and present, and a discussion of classroom practices, to encourage the creative spirit, are mandatory. An additional attribute for an effective book is a manner of writing indicative of an experienced and sensitive personality. George Horn ably fulfills these requirements within his endeavor. Considerable background as a classroom teacher and an administrator combined with a keen aesthetic viewpoint, derived from long exposure with the arts, has provided the author with strong credentials.

Leaf through this publication. Sense its range and quality. Notice the diversity of forms, a primitive mask, a seventeenth century etching, a painting of the present, even a future plan for a city. Or consider the suggestions for carving material and constructing in clay, or the treatment of color or textile designing, even the visual relationships of advertising. These comprise but a few of the considerations within these pages.

To discern the role of art has long concerned man. The Greek Plato spoke of art as the foundation for a beautiful society. And twentieth century man pursues the dream. For Berenson, as well as others, still contends that art, in its fullest sense should plan, build, and furnish this house of life. Perhaps it is the duty of teachers to encourage this view. And students must come to realize that every era, indeed each generation, must bear the responsibility of planning and erecting its own original monuments. George Horn's book reveals the nature of such monuments which can assist students in visualizing and committing themselves towards forms yet to come.

Thrusts of science are outward, directed towards the stars. Art involves an inward journey to the heart. In this technological age beset by computer and conformity, individualism must be retained. For man must never lose his inner eye or relinquish his unique voice. Otherwise all is lost. Thus inner challenge and noble quest remain prime aspects within the arts. Perhaps, in part, these are the intentions of this book.

James A. Schinneller
University of Wisconsin

INTRODUCTIONS

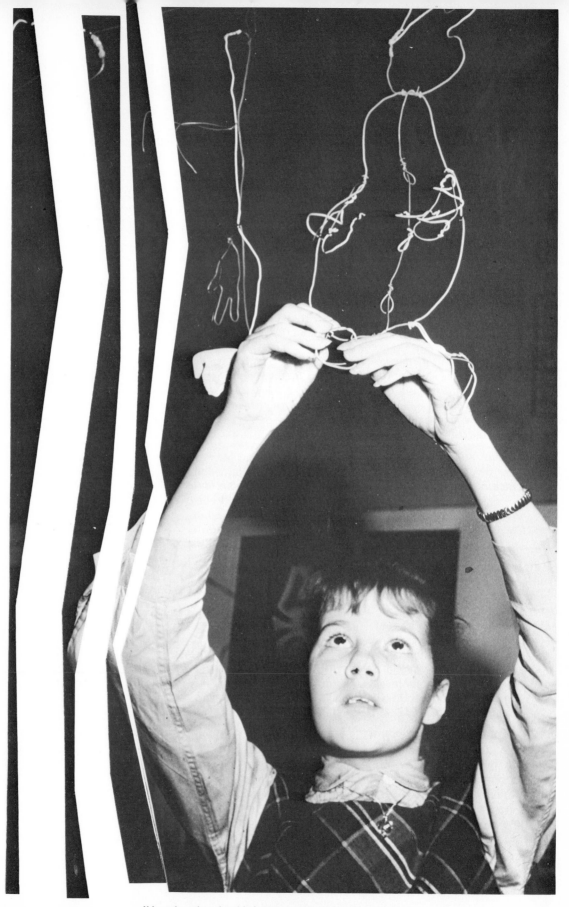

"Art education should aim to meet the demands of students
for both appreciation and production"—L. L. Winslow.

*This book is dedicated to
Dr. Leon L. Winslow,
pioneer and national leader
in art education, author,
painter, good friend.*

Experiences in art should speak to the student's capacity for inquiry, his accommodation for delight and wonder, and his joy of personal accomplishment . . .

. . . in his search for new meanings through materials.

*Plaster and vermiculite sculpture, Florida State University
School, Tallahassee.*

9

. . . in his reflection on his own
world of experiences.

Brush and ink drawing, Dade County public schools, Florida.

Plaster carving, Baltimore City public schools, Maryland.

. . . in his discovery of self.

Through confrontation with the product of the artist, the designer, the craftsman, the student's awareness of the immutable principles of unity, harmony, balance, line, shape, color, and texture may be heightened significantly. In addition, the blessings of art, providing insight into past civilizations and present concerns, are not to be denied. Nor can art's role in contributing elements of grandeur to our urban environments, in terms of order and visual joy, be overlooked. For this endeavor of art can provide significance to all the dwelling places of man.

Polyester plastic panel, Wolfgang Behl; courtesy American Craftsmen's Council, New York City.

Pedestal chair; courtesy Knoll Associates, Inc., New York.

13

Light; courtesy of Georg Jenson, Inc., New York City.

Textile design, Herman Miller.

CBS Building, New York City.

17

Handcrafted wood doors of hanging cabinet, John Kapel;
courtesy Pasadena Art Museum, California.

Detail from "Drowned Echo," Luba Krejci; courtesy of the
American Craftsmen's Council, New York.

"Immolation", epoxy and plexiglass print, John B. Mitchell.

"Contrapunto", *18-foot stainless steel sculpture by*
Beverly Pepper. Commissioned by William Kaufman
Organization for the United States Plywood Building,
777 Third Ave., New York City.

20

KLINE

SIDNEY JANIS 15 EAST 57 NEW YORK
19 MAY THROUGH 14 JUNE 1958

Poster, Franz Kline; courtesy of Poster Originals, Limited, New York.

Metal fireplace; courtesy of Fire Drum Corporation, California. Designer, Gerald L. Jonas.

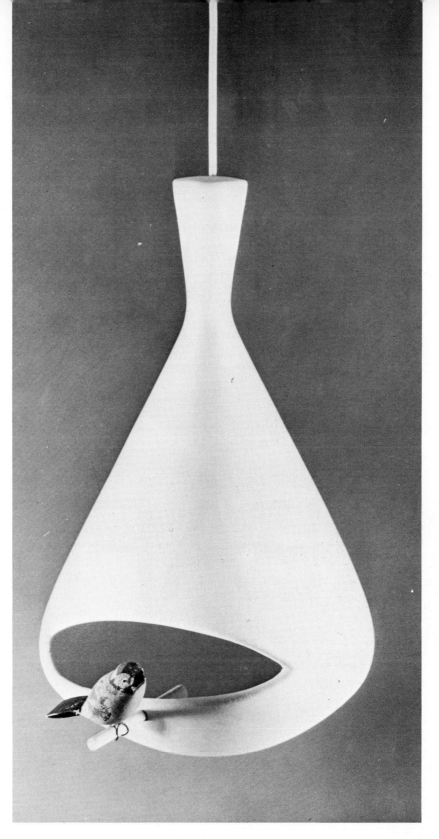

Ceramic bird house; courtesy of Architectural Pottery Corporation, Los Angeles, California.

SHEAFFER

Corporate mark and logotype of W. A. Sheaffer Pen Co.
Designed by Lippincott and Margulies, Inc., New York.

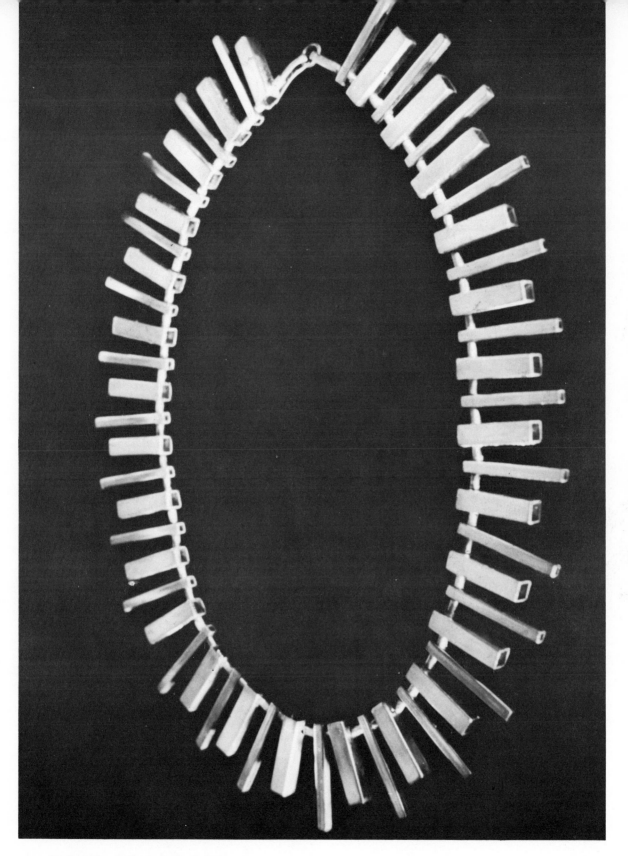

Sterling silver collar by Sarita R. Rainey.

Metal sculpture, front of 200 E. 42nd Street, New York City; by H. Jack Schainen and Alfred Charles Stern. Photo courtesy Peter Askins, Durst Organization, New York.

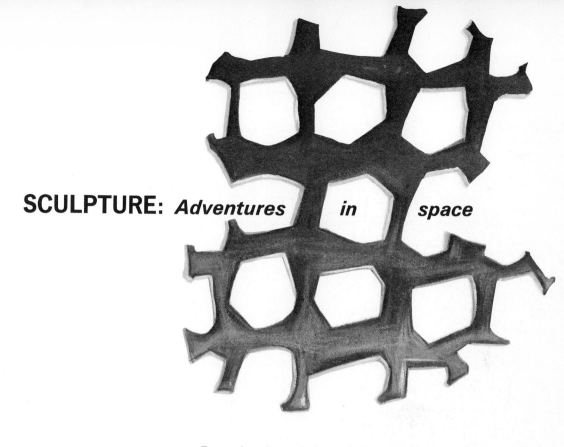

SCULPTURE: *Adventures in space*

From the time of the bulging Venuses, carved during the Stone Age some 30,000 years ago, until present day, man has produced an endless stream of three-dimensional configurations that have survived the elements to provide us with a greater insight into the religious, social, and political life of past cultures. Tiny figurines in honor of the gods, sophisticated Sumerian friezes, the monumental Sphinx of Gizeh, the superb achievement of the Greek Phidias, the aesthetic maturity of primitive Negro carvings, and a profusion of additional examples attest to man's fascination with three-dimensional materials as a means of visual expression.

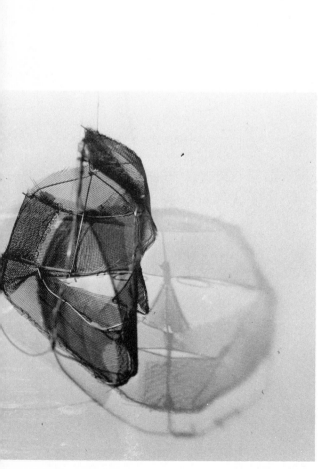

Head, wire and wire screening, Baltimore City public schools, Maryland.

27

Seated figure of a warrior, Pre-Columbian sculpture, Totonac Culture, probably San Andres Tuxtla, late period, terra cotta. The Baltimore Museum of Art, Maryland.

Until a relatively recent point on the scale of recorded history, sculpture could be described more or less as an organization of solid masses and volumes. While this may appear as an over-simplification, it is true that the essential concern of the sculptor, prior to this century, was with solidity, identifying contours, planes, and various modifications of surfaces as he hammered, carved, and modeled in search of a form of his own liking in stone, wood, or clay. In-the-round, relief, and intaglio became familiar terms describing the three major techniques of the sculptor.

Stone cat mortar, Pre-Columbian sculpture, Mantano Culture, micaceous schist. The Baltimore Museum of Art, Maryland.

Colossal Head No. 1, sculptured from andesite rock, Olmec Culture, Mexico. 1st to 5th C., Height 2.75 meters, weight 14 tons; courtesy Instituto de Antropologia de la Universidad Veracruzana.

Influenced by various emerging art movements and receiving impetus from man's search for new meanings with materials, Twentieth Century three-dimensional design has acquired much broader connotations than the sculpture of tradition. Characterized by its openness of design, its utilization of non-conventional materials and techniques, and its emphasis on space as an important visual element within the design, today's sculpture often reflects a pleasing disregard for traditional sculptural procedures. Exciting, fresh, imaginative structures in various combinations of wire, string, metal, plastics, wood, scraps, and found objects have caught the spirit of technological change, social reform, and man's vault into outer reaches of the universe. Drilling, sawing, welding, soldering, gluing have become as much a part of the sculptor's studio as modeling and carving.

Of considerable significance is the more than modest impact of the Twentieth Century sculptor on the products of industry and on contemporary architecture. Although there is a great deal to be desired in this respect, many manufacturers of furniture, household appliances, tools, toys, and countless other items are showing a greater sensitivity for good sculptural form in their products. Engaging sculptured pieces are appearing with greater frequency on the exteriors and in the lobbies and reception rooms of sleek new office buildings.

Architectural model of bronze wall sculpture on travertine base, by Roger Daricarrere; courtesy Pasadena Art Museum, California.

Model of carved cement sculpture for a dormitory at Yale University, New Haven, Connecticut. Eero Saarinen, Architect; courtesy American Craftsmen's Council, New York.

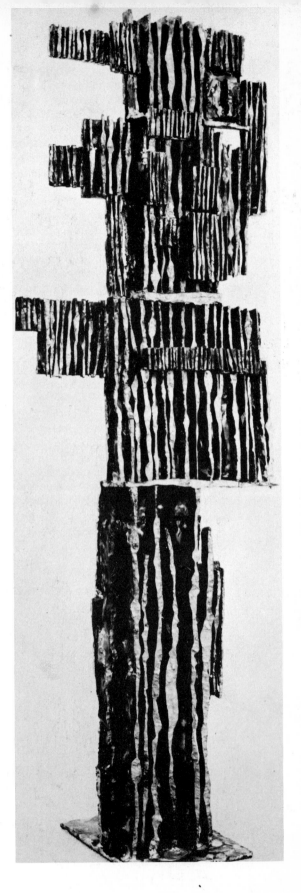

The Decalcomanie Queen (Crossover No. 8), welded bronze and copper sculpture by Abraham Schiemowitz; courtesy American Craftsmen's Council, New York.

Three-dimensional wall sculpture of various types of veneer wood by William Bowie. Displayed on corridor walls of the United States Plywood Building, New York City; courtesy United States Plywood Corporation.

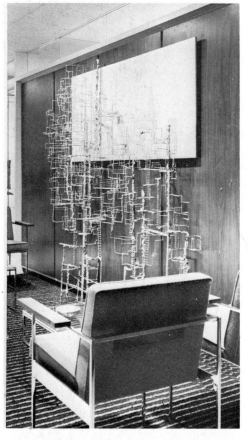

Sculpture for reception room, Durst Organization, New York, by H. Jack Schainen and Alfred Charles Stern, New York.

Sculpture, lobby of Lorillard Building, New York, by H. Jack Schainen and Alfred Charles Stern, New York.

31

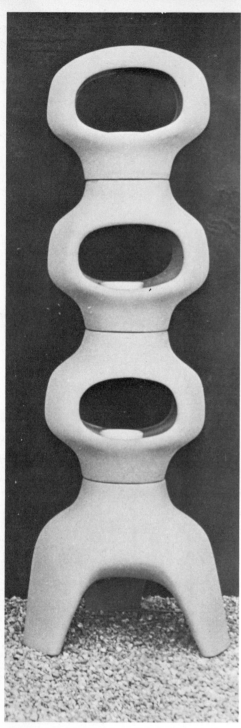

Ceramic light designed by Architectural Pottery, Los Angeles, California.

Ceramic divider, designed by Architectural Pottery, Los Angeles, California.

Walnut and aluminum animals, handcrafted by Douglas Moryl; courtesy Pasadena Art Museum, California.

Concrete pottery by Elsie Crawford,
Palo Alto, California.

Bertoia chair; courtesy Knoll Associates, Inc., New York.

Sculptured floor light by Elsie Crawford,
Palo Alto, California.

TWENTIETH CENTURY INFLUENCES

Although exposure to sculpture of the past will assist the student in his understanding of the role of sculpture in the history of man, the emphasis here will be on some of the influences, innovations, and personalities associated with Twentieth Century three-dimensional design. This is not to minimize the importance of our sculptural heritage but is an effort to focus the attention on the timely nature of this form of visual expression. It is suggested that sufficient time be allotted in the art program to give consideration to outstanding examples of sculpture throughout history.

While the efforts of the Cubists exercised a measure of influence on the sculptor, perhaps the most significant movement of this century was that of the Constructivists in 1913. Led by Tatlin, Naum Gabo, and Antoinne Pevsner, the Constructivists created sculptural forms that issued an invitation to the observer to enter them visually, to see them in their entirety from any angle. Combining plastics, wire, string, metal, and other heretofore non-conventional sculptural materials, **these artists achieved an interaction within the** sculptural form between space (open volume) and mass (solid volume). Thus, the shaping or building of sculptural forms placed equal importance on open space and solid areas.

Three years later another movement that has exerted considerable influence on the artist of the Twentieth Century was born. Originally founded in Zurich, Switzerland by Tristan Tzara and Andre Breton, Dadaism was subsequently developed by Jean Arp and a group of artists in France. Their work was thought of as a protest against society as well as a rebellion against man's destruction of himself. The public's reaction may be summed up in its reference to the artists as madmen. More important, however, the Dada movement advanced a fascinating new art concept, the *collage* (first introduced by Cubists) ranging from paper and paste form to a woven fabric of various three-dimensional scraps. Perhaps even more characteristic of Dadaism was the notion of ready-mades, or the art of assemblage. In addition to Arp, such noted personalities as Man Ray, Marcel Duchamp, Kurt Schwitters, and Max Ernst were closely indentified with the movement.

Linear Construction, Variation. Plastic and thread construction, Naum Gabo, 1942; The Phillips Collection, Washington, D.C.

Merzbild 20A, Collage, Kurt Schwitters, 1919. A. E. Gallatin collection, Philadelphia Museum of Art.

Paralleling the abstract sculptures of the Constructivists and the pictorial plasticity of the Dadaists, the inimitable inventions of Alexander Calder added still another dimension to space investigation, mechanical movement. Calder's mobile, a singularly American art form, achieved actual movement by the manner in which its component parts were joined. These ingenious devices of Calder differed from the work of Gabo and others in that they assumed a sequence of identities through the continually changing relationships of space and shapes within a single construction.

The succeeding years have witnessed many variations on and deviations from these earlier concepts of Twentieth Century three-dimensional design. Yet the spirit of innovation and search reflected in the work of Gabo, Pevsner, Arp, Calder, and numerous others has been projected into many facets of today's society.

One of the greatest influences on the school art program in this respect was the Bauhaus School, organized in Germany shortly after World War I. The major objective of the Bauhaus was to train stylists and craftsmen for industry. The entire first year's experience for all students centered on the search of materials to discover new uses that may be adapted to the manufacturing process. Students were encouraged to explore, to invent, and to move beyond conventional design concepts in existence at that time.

The universally popular appeal of three-dimensional design in today's school art program attests to the exciting challenge provided by this form of visual expression. In addition to the more traditional carving and modeling techniques, constructing with cardboard, wood, wire, metal, plastics, paper, and seemingly unlimited combinations of materials and found objects has captured the imagination of the art student. The results of these adventures in space ordinarily are formed to stand on their own projections, to be anchored to a base, or to be suspended in mid-air. In some there may be a particular stress on linear quality; in others, the emphasis may be on interacting shapes, moving parts, or transparency of materials. Ideas based on natural or man-made forms, animals and figures in action, imagination and invention, span the range of interpretation from near-representation to pure abstraction.

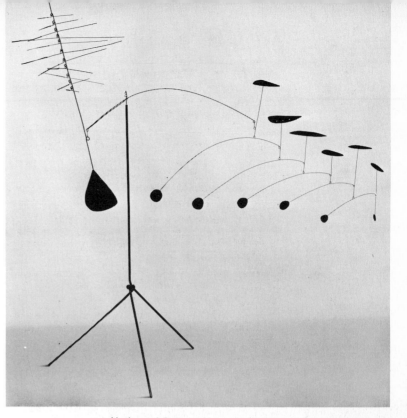

Horizontal Spines, Alexander Calder. In the collection of Addision Gallery, Phillips Academy, Andover, Massachusetts.

Molded plaster shapes mounted on wire fixed in a wood base; Baltimore City public schools, Maryland.

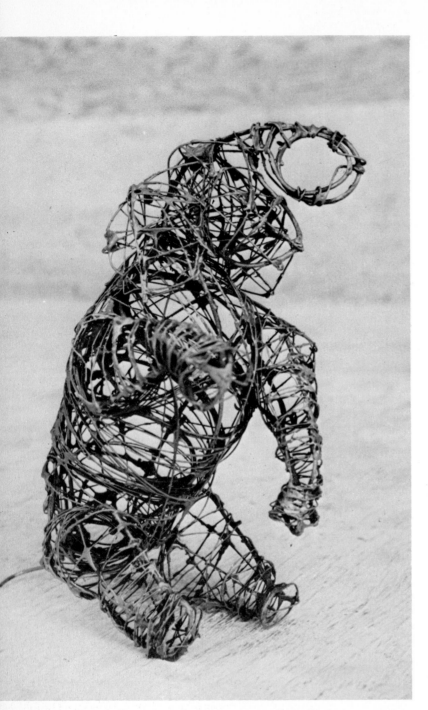

Wire sculpture; Lutheran High School, Los Angeles, California.

EMPHASES, MATERIALS, PROCEDURES

Unfortunately, three-dimensional problems often degenerate into complex tieing, bending, and gluing activities with little design value. This may occur when the student gets caught up in a maze of materials with instructions to be "creative." To avoid such a catastrophy, consideration should be given to sculpture as a form of expression throughout history, to contemporary trends and techniques in three-dimensional design, and to the influence of materials on sculptural form.

Familiarize the student with important sculpture of the past (prints, films, filmstrips, museum trips). What was the role of sculpture in ancient cultures? In what ways were materials a determining factor in the work of the sculptor? How did the social, political, and religious structure in various eras serve as forces on the efforts of the sculptor? What influence did the sculptor have on society? Discuss the significant sculptural trends of the Twentieth Century. Compare the work of the past with contemporary three-dimensional design. Point out the relationship of materials to treatment of sculptural form, interpretation of subject-matter or ideas; to mass, volume, open space, transparency; to textural qualities. This kind of an encounter with outstanding examples of three-dimensional design will assist the student toward a greater depth of understanding of sculpture as a prominent force in the history of man. It will broaden his concept of three-dimensional design as a means of personal expression. It will acquaint him with the essentials of design as they find application in three-dimensional forms. It will make him knowledgeable of the diversity of materials that have been adapted to three-dimensional expression.

Of considerable importance is the fact that three-dimensional design experiences provide the student an additional means for personal visual expression. Specific problems in carving, modeling, constructing, wire sculpture, and paper sculpture should be defined to encourage spontaneous effort and to foster an inquiring spirit. At the same time, the exciting process of designing with three-dimensional materials should contribute to the student's growing esthetic sensitivity. His discovery of unusual and interesting relationships of line, shape, space, color, value, and texture through new-found understandings of materials or combinations of materials should support the concept that visual organization (as opposed to disorder) is a basic ingredient of all art form. An awareness of the visual elements and a sensibility for the qualities of unified design along with a knowledge of the potential of various materials is as essential to the assembling of a mobile or the making of a three-dimensional construction as they are to the composition of a painting, the layout of a poster, or the plans for a contemporary house.

Three-dimensional design problems may be introduced with a single material (plaster block) to achieve a specific emphasis or they may be based on a combination of two or more materials (wood strips and colored construction paper) to obtain a variety of effects. Discuss with the student some of the inherent characteristics of various materials. For example, *wire* may be bent, twisted, coiled, balled, cut, soldered, hammered; *wood*, cut, carved, sawed, splintered, drilled, glued, nailed; *cardboard*, cut, scored, bent, glued, notched, slotted; *paper*, cut, folded, perforated, torn, wrinkled, slotted, glued, stapled; *plastic*, sawed, drilled, cast (liquid form), filed, sanded, cemented; *plaster*, carved, cast, applied over a structure in liquid form. Provide the student opportunity to handle materials through simple exploratory activities to become acquainted with the potential and limitations of materials.

Specific problems in three-dimensional design should be defined to set a direction for creative response. This may mean establishing certain limitations as to maximum or minimum size of the design, number of different materials that may be used in a single design; whether the design should stand on its own projections, be attached to a base, or be suspended; whether the design should include moving parts. When this is done, the stated problems will serve as a guide, providing the student a meaningful framework within which to seek his own personal answer.

A student may wish to prepare a preliminary sketch for the purpose of organizing his ideas, to establish an initial direction. It is desirable, however, to encourage an early association of idea with three-dimensional materials, since the materials themselves are a significant influence on the response of the student. As three-dimensional materials are being used they suggest certain possibilities or impose definite limitations on the student as he shapes his idea. Also, there is an entirely different kind of personal involvement with sculptural materials that does not exist in materials that are used ordinarily in the making of a preliminary sketch. Working directly with three-dimensional materials more often produces a desired freshness and intuitiveness in the design.

In summary, three-dimensional design activities should broaden the student's understanding of the role of sculpture in the past and present with an emphasis on trends and innovations of the Twentieth Century; should give the student opportunity to investigate a variety of three-dimensional materials and techniques; should emphasize quality in design and instill in the student a concern for good craftsmanship. By encouraging an imaginative, inventive attitude in the student, three-dimensional design experiences will provide him with meaningful adventures in space.

37

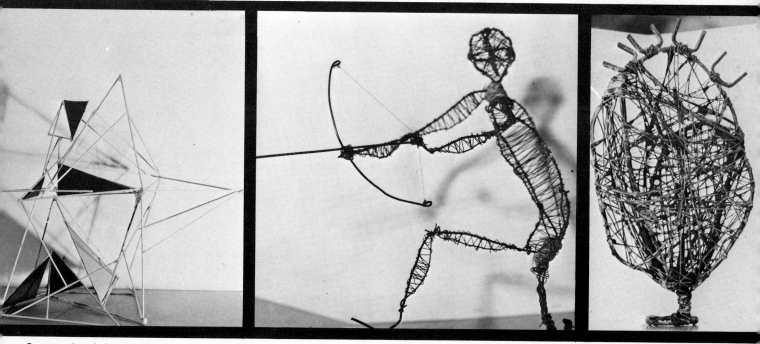

Construction, balsa wood strips and colored poster board shapes; Baltimore City public schools, Maryland.

Wire figure; Baltimore City public schools, Maryland.

Wire sculpture; Lutheran High School, Los Angeles, California.

Balsa strip construction mounted on a base; Kansas City public schools, Missouri.

Constructing

Design activities associated with the process of constructing are the delight of today's art student. This may be the result of the genuine sense of satisfaction that ordinarily evolves from the act of building. Or it may be the feeling of accomplishment that is achieved with the many kinds of materials associated with this facet of design. Then too, it would seem that wire sculptures, mobiles, stabiles, assemblages are fitting spokesmen for the age of space. Whatever the reason, this form of visual expression has indeed captured the imagination.

Problems in constructing may be quite simple and charming. They also may be rather complex, depending on the projected objectives and the experience, or the desire of the student. Designing with wire, for example, may be thought of as drawing in space. Wire, playing the role of line, may be bent to enclose space, to create a shape, to represent a figure, to give a feeling for action. Other materials may be combined with wire to establish closed areas, to create color and texture, to give mass and density. Shapes that move may be attached within the design or extended beyond its periphery as points of interest. Some three-dimensional problems may suggest building on a solid background, for example the arrangement of wood blocks of various sizes on a rectangular shape of plywood. Cardboard rectangles of different sizes, glued on end over a heavy cardboard background pose an interesting experiment in shape organization. The possibilities are unlimited!

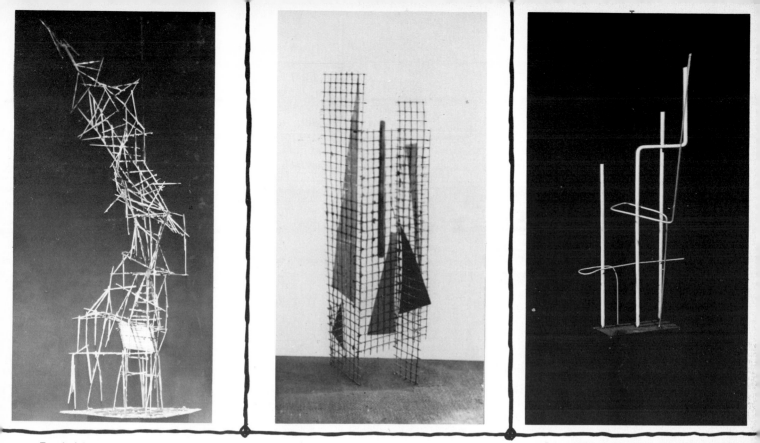

Toothpick construction; Baltimore City public schools, Maryland.

Acetate and mesh wire construction; Montclair public schools, New Jersey.

Wire construction; Baltimore City public schools, Maryland.

MATERIALS AND TOOLS

Wood of various widths and thicknesses, balsa wood strips and sheets, applicator sticks, reed, corks, toothpicks, blocks, wood scraps from a lumber yard or the industrial arts scrap box.

Varieties of paper, poster board, cardboard. Colored tissue, construction paper.

Plastics (clear and colored) of different thicknesses, acetate, cellophane, liquid plastic.

Stained glass.

Stove-pipe wire, bell wire, thin-gauge binding wire, welding rods (different weights and lengths), aluminum wire, lightweight coat-hanger wire, wire mesh.

Sheet tin, aluminum, copper, metal foils.

Liquid or paste metal (Sculpmetal), plaster, sand, asbestos, asbestos cement.

String, thread, yarn, twine.

Scraps, junk, gears, nuts, bolts, found objects, cardboard boxes and containers (many sizes), mailing tubes, pebbles and stones, straws.

Fast-drying cement, paste, rubber cement, poly vinyl acetate, solder, nails, staples, straight pins.

Cardboard and balsa construction based on the theme, Street Signs; Baltimore City public schools.

The tools are determined by the materials and the processes that are basic to the problem. Many softer materials may require little more than the agile hands of the student. A basic list of tools, however, would include drills, cutting knives, files, rasps, coping saws, scissors, staplers, straight edges, glass cutters for stained glass, round nose pliers, cutting pliers, hack saws, jewelry saws, tin shears, soldering irons, torches.

Model for a playground structure, balsa wood and card-board; Lutheran High School, Los Angeles, California.

Integration of plastic shapes; Baltimore City public schools, Maryland.

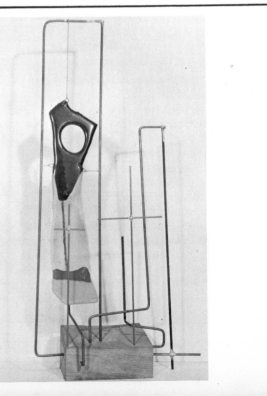

Wire structure with colored glass shape center of interest; Baltimore City public schools, Maryland.

EMPHASES, IDEAS AND DIRECTIONS

Because of the vast array of materials that have become associated with three-dimensional design activities and the diversity of directions that constructing may take, it is difficult to generalize on the design essentials that should be emphasized. Specific problem objectives should indicate the degree of emphasis on line, shape, form, mass, volume and the surface qualities color, value, texture. A construction based on wire may on one hand have characteristics that are predominantly linear. The introduction of cardboard or glass shapes to the same problem would bring about shape and possibly color relationships that would be quite important. In mobile design the student is concerned with mechanical as well as optical balance, shape and color relationships, and sometimes distinct line qualities. The making of a wire animal may place the attention of the student on volume or mass plus action. Thus, three-dimensional constructing experiences involve the student in the unified organization of the visual elements, yet with varying degrees of emphasis on particular elements. His awareness and understanding of basic design qualities, such as unity, balance, simplicity, movement, dominance and subordination, will serve to make this experience more meaningful.

Discuss with the student the influence of the ultimate environment of the design on its appearance, the effect of natural light, the use of strategically positioned artificial light to produce interesting patterns of shadows. How would the environment influence the use of color on the shapes of a mobile or the selection of materials for a stabile? By altering the background behind an object (large sheets of colored paper) the factor of environmental influence can be clarified. Student problems in constructing should be presented to encourage a feeling for freedom and spontaneity, an inquiring spirit. A well-defined problem will provide the student with a definite framework in which he may explore his ideas with certain materials. In addition to the projected goals, a problem should be stated to include limitations on the number of different materials to be used, maximum and minimum size of the design, whether the design should have moving parts or not, whether it should be made to stand alone, on a base, be suspended in space, or to be displayed on a background. There are undoubtedly other factors that may be considered as a part of the problem definition. Of significance is that the statement is formulated in such a way that it will open up avenues for meaningful student search.

Toothpick construction in artificially lighted environment; Baltimore City public schools, Maryland.

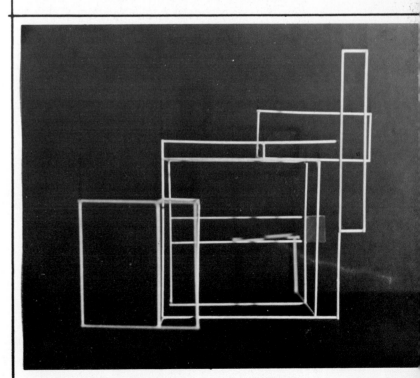

Applicator stick form against a dark background; Baltimore City public schools, Maryland.

41

Exposure of the student to good examples of contemporary design through museum visits, good examples of contemporary architecture in the community (newer architectural concepts and structures which reflect the spirit of contemporary design; buildings having sculptured pieces as a part of their exteriors and interiors), trips to the zoo or farm (animal wire sculpture), study of natural forms (trees, twigs, weeds, flowers, seed pods), appropriate films, filmstrips and reproductions of Twentieth Century sculpture, will serve as sources for student ideas. Encourage the student to carry a sketch book to record ideas on the spot. The study and sketching of action figures in the art room, on the athletic field, the playground and other parts of the school and community is a good preliminary to wire sculpture figures. Then, too, ideas often grow out of an experimental search of materials. Conduct classroom discussions of these experiences. How may they be developed in three-dimensional form. Consider the appropriateness of materials to idea. Stress good workmanship, inventiveness.

Sketching with felt pen, soft charcoal, black crayon on large sheets of newsprint, the student will have opportunity to search for ideas, to set up varying space and shape relationships, to seek different kinds of action, movement, and unity in his design. However, an early association of idea with three-dimensional materials is important. The student should be encouraged to move from sketch to three-dimensional materials with an open mind. The inherent qualities of the materials themselves will be influential on his idea as he shapes it into a unified organization. Often the completed construction will be quite different from the pre-sketched design concept.

42

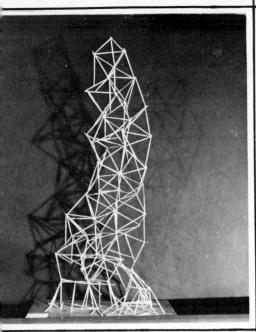

Toothpick sculpture based on the repeated unit; Baltimore City public schools, Maryland.

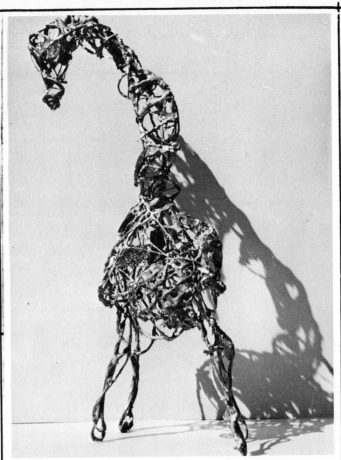

Wire and Sculpmetal giraffe; Lutheran High School, Los Angeles, California.

43

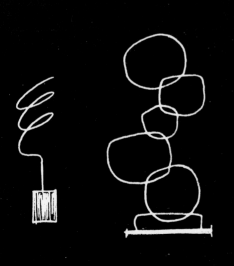

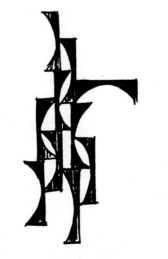

Wire sculpture developed from a single strand of aluminum wire; Montclair public schools, New Jersey.

TYPICAL PROBLEMS

Non-objective design based on single length of soft wire, six feet in length. (Use masking tape on ends as a protective measure.) Design to stand on its own projections. Emphasize linear qualities, movement, enclosure of space, depth as well as height and width.

This problem may be modified to suggest the use of straight lines and ninety degree bends only; curved lines only; the addition of liquid metal to create weight, mass, and textural effects; the attaching of one end of the wire to a wood block and developing the design with the block serving as a counter-balancing factor; cutting the wire into short pieces and re-integrating it by soldering.

Action figures, animals, fish, birds, bugs; materials organized in groups: (1) various weights of wire; (2) wire and liquid metal; (3) wire, cloth, and plaster; (4) wire, cardboard, liquid metal. Sports, caricatures, crazy birds, imaginative animals, a ''zoo's who.'' Emphasize action, spirit, simplification rather than precise detail. Discuss different techniques: single strand of wire (contour-like), several strands to suggest volume, balling wire to create mass, coiling wire for springy effects, heavy wire for structure and finer wire for building up.

This problem may be modified to include found objects, colored construction paper, yarn; groups of figures.

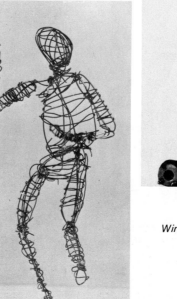

Wire bug; Lutheran High School, Los Angeles, California.

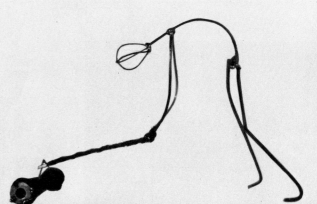

Wire figures; Baltimore City public schools, Maryland.

44

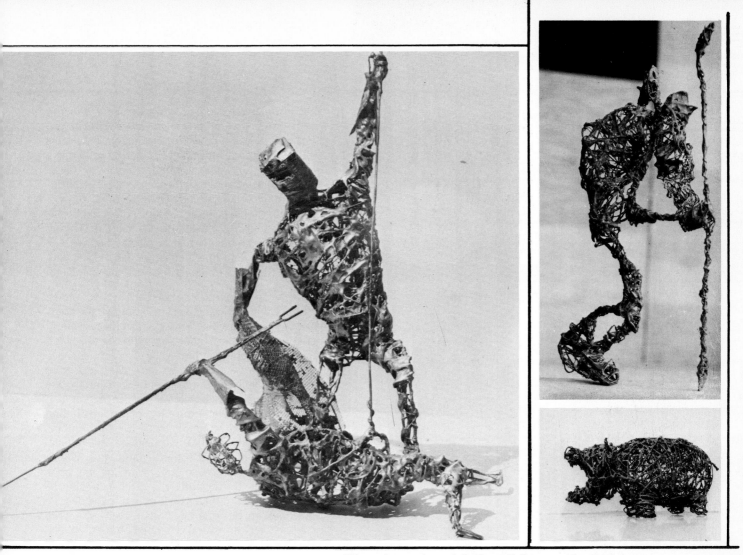

Wire, wire mesh, and Sculpmetal figures and animals;
Lutheran High School, Los Angeles, California.

Balled wire figure; Baltimore City
public schools, Maryland.

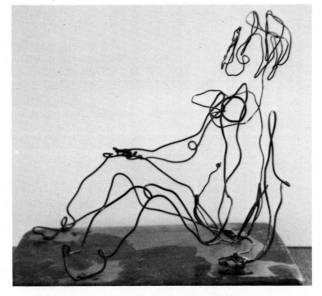

Wire figure; Montclair public schools, New Jersey.

Plaster forms attached to wire rods; Baltimore City public schools, Maryland.

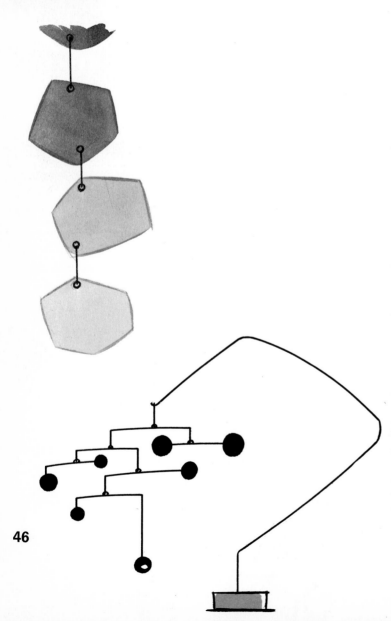

Wire and plaster forms; coathanger wire, welding rods, plaster, modeling clay, small cardboard boxes. Suggest the creation of interesting plaster forms mounted on wire supports which are attached to a wood base. Discuss characteristics of basic shapes and possible variations, shape relationships, unity of design, articulation of 3, 5, or 7 related shapes in a single design. Consider possibilities for making plaster shapes such as pouring plaster in small boxes, half of a small hollow ball, depressions made in a slab of modeling clay with fingers or objects, hollows pressed into wet sand.

Mobiles. Lightweight coathangers, welding rods, armature wire, stove-pipe wire, balsa strips, lightweight wood dowels, poster board, heavyweight construction paper, sheet aluminum or tin, nylon threads, fast-drying glue. NOTE: Mobiles have been misinterpreted possibly more than any other single art form. Student products often are nothing more than unrelated shapes hanging in space. This results from lack of understanding of the essential characteristics of the mobile. Discuss the importance of delicate mechanical balance of the component parts to achieve natural, graceful movement. Mobiles are constructed from the bottom up. The balancing of each part is determined as it is added to the design. Some mobile designs are constructed with wire or wood strip arms and attached shapes; others, with shapes alone.

Emphasize the use of simple basic shapes and variations, a single shape (various sizes) throughout the design. Although interesting shapes may be derived from nature, discourage the use of trite realistic shapes (fish, stars, leaves). Suggest the use of a single color with a contrasting color for an accent; or the use of different values of a single color. Suggest that the student experiment with eight or ten similar shapes balanced and joined with nylon thread. Discuss the influence of light and the surrounding area on the design. Discuss the importance of linear movement and direction when using wire or wood strip arms in the mobile. Wire arms should be free of kinks and ripples. Welding rods $\frac{1}{16}$" in diameter are excellent for arms. Encourage the student to explore various methods for joining component parts to get different effects.

47

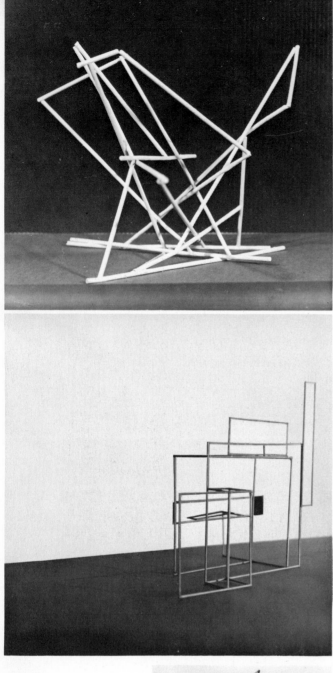

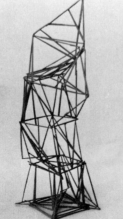

Designs developed with toothpicks, applicator sticks, or straws. Using any of these materials suggests that the student build a design by integrating a number of basic units into a single design. Discuss the possible variations that may be achieved in the articulation of 7, 9, 11 or more units into a unified organization.

In addition to these few examples of typical problems, the illustrations included here suggest many other types of problems which involve the student in the process of constructing. Some stress the use of wood as the basic structural element; others, found objects and junk; toothpicks and reed formed in a curvilinear fashion; wood scraps; wire and wire mesh; cardboard and paper.

It might be added here that there is a close relationship between constructing experiences and architectural design, interior design, product design, and industrial design. Follow-up activities to be considered may include the design of space or room dividers, storage walls, lighting, toys, puzzles, displays, packaging, jewelry, furniture, outdoor sculpture (fountains, bird baths, hanging ornaments), tools, utensils, and playground equipment.

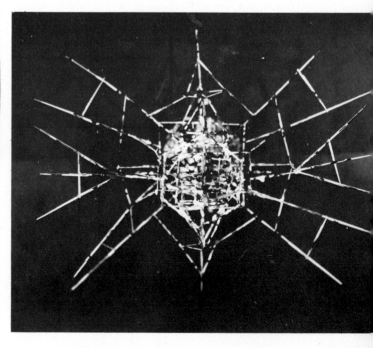

Constructions using straws, applicator sticks, and toothpicks; Baltimore City public schools, Maryland.

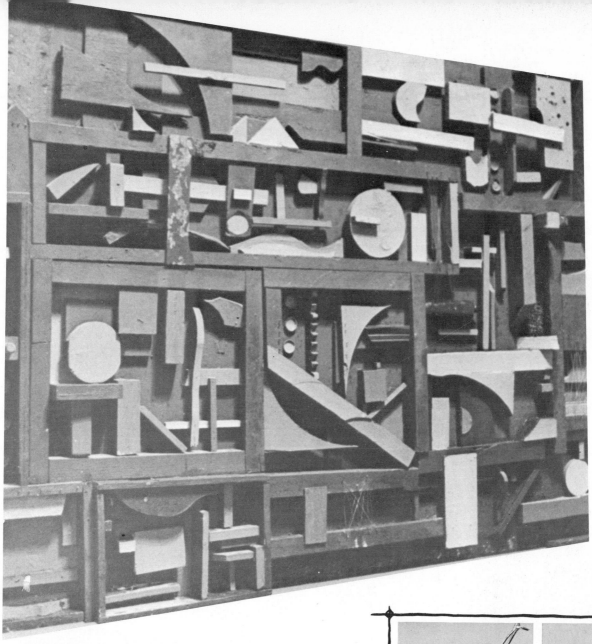

"Composition 4", construction; Dade County public schools, Florida. Photo courtesy Miami Museum of Modern Art.

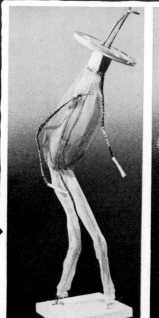

Figures; Baltimore City public schools, Maryland.

ASSEMBLAGE

Automobile, assemblage; Bridgeport public schools, Connecticut.

Assemblage; Dade County public schools, Florida. Photo courtesy Miami Museum of Modern Art.

Metal on wood base; Montclair public schools, New Jersey.

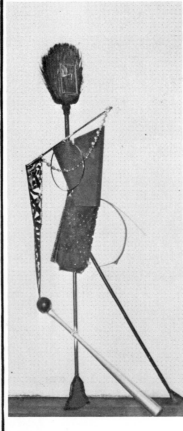

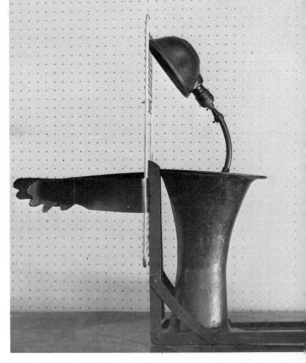

Ballplayers, assemblage; Bridgeport public schools, Connecticut.

Foam glass sculpture; Florida State University School, Tallahassee, Florida.

Carving and Modeling

Both carving and modeling activities provide another facet to the student's experience in three-dimensional design. These two techniques have been a part of the sculptor from the earliest of times. Carving, or sculpting, is principally the process of cutting away from a block or a solid mass, while modeling is the act of building a form or adding to, with a plastic material.

There are many different kinds of materials that should be considered for student projects. Some may be used in their natural form, such as wood or clay; others may be prepared, such as a combination of plaster and sand or a quantity of papier-mâché. Some man-made materials, such as fire brick or wax blocks, lend themselves to sculptural activities. An emphasis should be placed on the importance of observing the natural qualities of the material, whatever it may be.

Materials such as a plaster block or wet clay, require no more tools than a paring knife, sticks, and the student's hands. On the other hand, carving in stone would call for special hammers, mallets, and an assortment of steel tools or chisels that are made especially for this purpose.

Figure, plaster; Baltimore City public schools, Maryland.

Hippopotamus, plaster and vermiculite; Baltimore City public schools, Maryland.

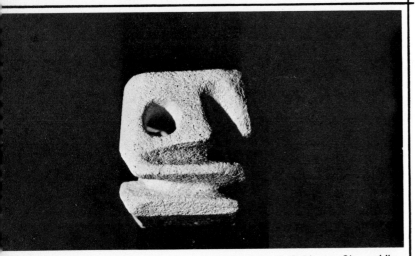

Non-objective, plaster and sand; Baltimore City public schools, Maryland.

MATERIALS AND TOOLS

CARVING

Firebrick, Foam Glass Blocks, Wax Blocks, Clay Blocks, may be carved with paring knives, stencil knives, large nails, sticks.

Plaster poured into cardboard cartons to form block may be carved with ordinary knives, sticks, large nails, sculpture tools.

Mixtures—(1) Plaster and vermiculite in equal quantities. (2) One part plaster and two parts sand. (3) One part plaster, one part cement, one part sand, four parts vermiculite. (4) One part sand, one part cement, three parts vermiculite. In each of these mixtures, the materials should be mixed thoroughly, water added, and then poured into desired container to harden. India ink, vegetable colors, dry or liquid tempera may be added to give color. Also sawdust may be added to the plaster to produce a harder block.

Cork carves easily with knives.

Wood of many varieties, such as cherry, walnut, apple, pine, may be carved with wood chisels, gouges, veining tools, knives. Rasps, files, sandpaper, may be used to produce the desired finish. Wood logs and driftwood often suggest a design with little carving required.

Wax Blocks, clear or in colors, may be carved with a knife.

Stone ordinarily requires stone carving hammers and mallets, steel sculpture chisels and tools. Some stones or rock chunks suggest a sculptural form that necessitates little carving to bring out the idea. Soapstone is a soft material that may be carved with a paring knife.

MODELING

Plasticine, an oil base clay, is perhaps one of the widest used modeling materials. The warmth of the hands will soften plasticine, and the student's fingers are his best tools. However, there are many shapes and forms of sculpture tools available for working with plasticine. Different sizes of sticks will serve the purpose. Commercially-made, adjustable armatures for figures and animals may be obtained through local art dealers. The student may make his own armature, using wire mounted on a heavy wood block. The size of the figure would determine the weight of the wire.

Animals, cork; Florida State University School, Tallahassee, Florida.

Wet clay, ranging from low-firing clay bodies to high-firing natural clays, ready for use, is available through local art suppliers. Usually white, red, or buff, wet clay objects may be decorated, glazed and fired. (See suggestions for surface treatment under ''Ceramics.'') Modeling techniques should include pinch, coil, and slab procedures. Grog, ground firebrick, may be added to wet clay to produce special textured effects. Plastic bags may be placed over wet clay to prevent drying between work periods.

Papier-mâché for puppet heads, figures or animals may be made by shredding newspaper, soaking in water, draining water, adding wheat paste until it is to the consistency of soft modeling clay. A few drops of oil of cloves may be added to prevent spoilage. Asbestos pulp may be used instead of newspaper. Papier-mâché may be modeled over a wire armature, a cardboard form, wood structure, bottles, old light bulbs (heads). The papier-mâché strip method of modeling is simply the dipping of strips of newspaper into wheat paste and placing them over a form until the desired thickness is reached. Wheat paste added to

sawdust or wood shavings forms a modeling material that is most suitable for mask making.

Casting with plaster over clay relief designs, cut and torn pieces of heavy cardboard arranged and glued to the bottom of a tray with sides, or over a design pressed or modeled in a container of wet sand, provides the student additional interesting sculptural experiences. This experience may be extended to the making of multi-sectioned molds from modeled figures and the casting of duplicates. Space does not allow thorough discussion of the process here but several good books are mentioned in the references.

Many additional commercially-prepared materials, such as Sculp-metal and Pariscraft may be considered for carving and modeling activities. Sculp-metal is a liquid or paste form of metal that may be modeled on a wire armature or applied over most any material (cardboard, paper, plaster, wood). When it dries, Sculp-metal may be carved, filed, burnished. Pariscraft, plaster-coated gauze, when wet may be draped or modeled over a structure or form. These materials are available ordinarily through local art dealers.

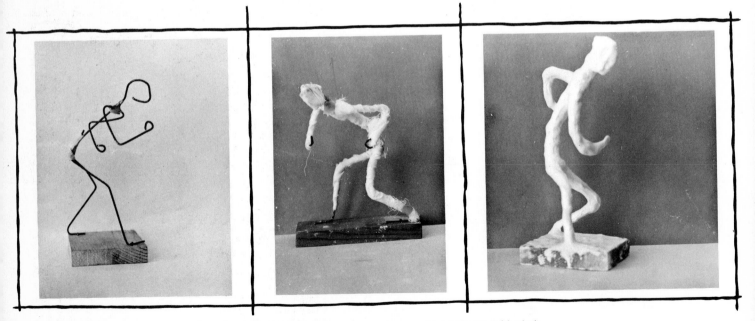

Modeling with wet plaster over a wire armature built up with cloth.

54

Figure modeled in wet clay; Montclair public schools, New Jersey.

Animal, papier-mâché; Baltimore City public schools, Maryland.

Don Quixote, plaster on wire; Dade County public schools, Florida.

55

IDEAS

Sketching trips, museum visits, films, prints of examples of sculpture of the past and present may be used as a means of assisting the student in his search for ideas. What is suggested by the unusual lines in a stone, the movements of a cat, the upward sweep of a tree? Have the student sketch figures in action, in the school, the community, his home—sports, social events, or just everyday scenes. Perhaps he would like to design a fountain for a garden, a decorative piece (scaled down) for the front of an office building, or a simple design to serve as an accent in a room. Figures, groups of figures, heads, animals, totems, puppets, masks, any of these may form a basis for the student's expression in three dimensions. A plaster block may suggest a non-objective design, a free form. Odds and ends and a variety of found objects (gears, screws, bolts, junk) may be used to form a basis for a sand casting. Encourage the student to use his imagination, to experiment with ideas.

The student may work directly with carving or modeling materials or he may pre-sketch his ideas. Emphasize interest or appeal of the idea, good visual organization, the unusual, careful workmanship. Suggest that with most sculptural materials he should aim for simplicity, avoid delicate details, take advantage of the natural qualities of the materials. Figures or animals in-the-round should be built to stand alone; should show action.

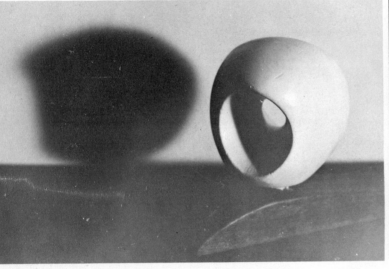

Carved plaster form mounted on wood base; Baltimore City public schools, Maryland.

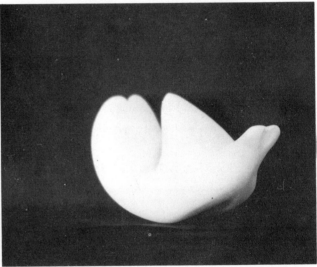

Carved plaster form; Vancouver public schools, Washington.

Carved plaster form; Anne Arundel County public schools, Maryland.

56

Figure carved in plaster; Frederick County public schools, Maryland.

Sand casting; Bridgeport public schools, Connecticut.

Non-objective designs carved in plaster blocks; Montclair public schools, New Jersey.

Carved plaster form; Baltimore City public schools, Maryland.

57

CARVING IN WOOD

Washington County public schools, Maryland.

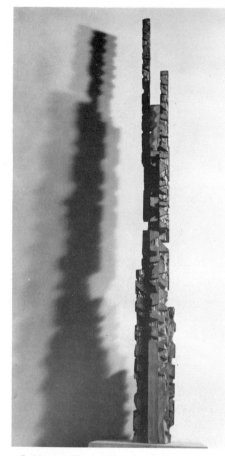

Baltimore City public schools, Maryland.

Baltimore City public schools, Maryland.

58

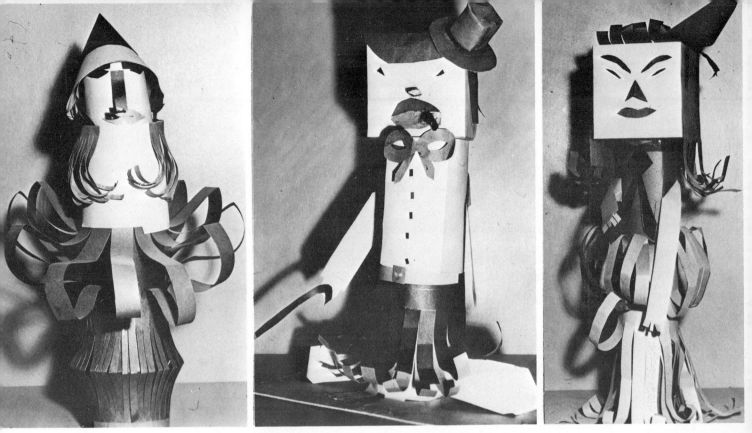

Paper sculpture figures, Baltimore City public schools, Maryland.

Clown Head; from the book, "Paper Sculpture", by Mary Grace Johnston.

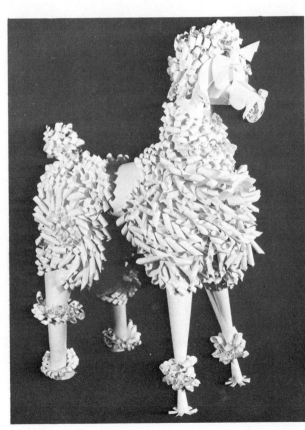

French Poodle; from the book, "Paper Sculpture", by Mary Grace Johnston.

PAPER SCULPTURE

Bronze mask, African, possibly Yoruba, Nigeria. The Baltimore Museum of Art, Wurtzburger collection of African art.

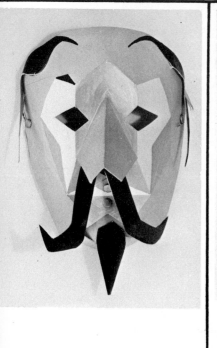

Wood mask, Ivory Coast of Africa. The Baltimore Museum of Art, Wurtzburger collection of African art.

Papier-mâché masks shaped over modeling clay forms; Baltimore City public schools, Maryland.

Paper sculpture masks by Elsie Crawford, Palo Alto, California.

61

Stone carving; Washington County public schools, Maryland.

Plaster; Montclair public schools, New Jersey.

Figure carved in firebrick; Bridgeport public schools, Connecticut.

62

Construction; Scotia-Glenville public schools, New York.

VARIOUS MEDIA

Balsa strips and colored tissue; Memphis public schools, Tennessee.

Toothpicks and colored cellophane; Scotia-Glenville public schools, New York.

Bird and wire cat; Baltimore City public schools, Maryland.

Wood carving; Frederick County public schools, Maryland.

63

Papier-mâché animals; Baltimore City public schools, Maryland.

Wire and Sculpmetal rooster; Lutheran High School, Los Angeles, California.

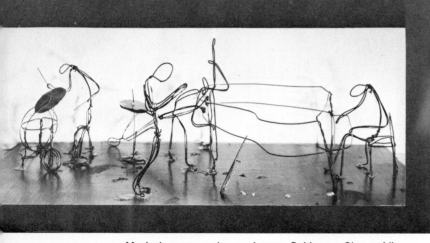

Musical group, wire sculpture; Baltimore City public schools, Maryland.

Ceramic clay figure; Vancouver public schools, Washington.

64

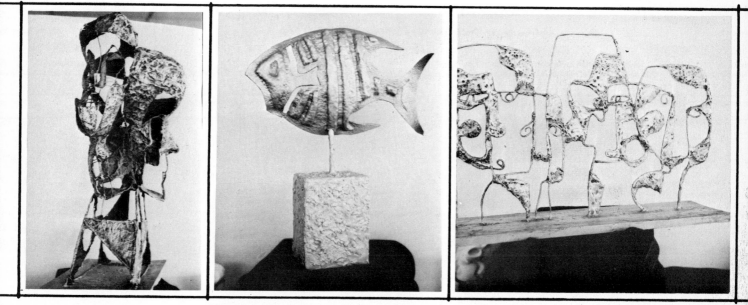

Metal sculptures; Prince Georges County public schools, Maryland.

SUGGESTED REFERENCES:

Creative Paper Design

Rottger, Ernst, Reinhold Publishing Corp., New York, 1961.
A well-illustrated reference presenting numerous examples of how paper can be pieced, cut, pasted, folded, and inter-woven into interesting forms and objects.

Sculpture: Techniques in Clay, Wax, Slate

Eliscu, Frank, Chilton Co.—Book Division, Philadelphia and New York, 1959.
Contains hundreds of photographs that clearly delineate the fundamental processes of sculpture with clay, wax, slate; good presentation of casting particularly jewelry and small objects by the lost-wax centrifugal process.

Ceramic Sculpture

Ford, Betty Davenport, Reinhold Publishing Corp., New York, 1964.
Excellent visualization of procedures in ceramic sculpture—animal, human, plant, and abstract forms; appropriate tools, clays and their preparation, idea sources; presents hollow, slab, and coil construction; firing procedures.

The Art of Assemblage

Seitz, William C., The Museum of Modern Art, 1961.

Sculpture and Ideas

Andrews, Michael, Prentice Hall, Inc., Englewood Cliffs, New Jersey, 1965.

Design In Three Dimensions

Randall, Reino and Haines, Edward C., Davis Publications, Inc., Worcester, Mass., 1965.

Paper Sculpture (Revised and Enlarged)

Johnston, Mary Grace, Davis Publications, Inc., Worcester, Mass., 1965.

Puppet Making Through the Grades

Hopper, Grizella H., Davis Publications, Inc., Worcester, Mass., 1966.

Exploring Papier-Mâché (Revised)

Betts, Victoria Bedford, Davis Publications, Inc., Worcester, Mass., 1966.

Lino cut, Dade County public schools, Florida.

PRINTMAKING: *Multiplying images*

The process of duplicating a design by transferring it from a prepared surface to another material may be traced back to the ancient Egyptians. The Chinese excelled in printing from wood and incised stone. Several centuries ago the Japanese produced sensitive, multicolored prints characterized by their supremely simplified composition. These prints, at first, were made from a single block and then colored by hand. Later, the Japanese developed the technique of printing from polychromed blocks.

While no attempt will be made here to chronologize prints, there are many outstanding practices of the art, past and present, that should be brought to the attention of the student. For comparative purposes, a list of examples may include the masterful etchings of Rembrandt, the religious and allegorical engravings of Albrecht Durer, the work of Martin Schongauer, the vivid commentaries on political and social life in the lithographs of Honore Daumier; and more recently the vigorous etchings, lithographs, and woodcuts of Kathe Kollwitz; the influence of African Primitivism reflected in the woodcuts of Karl Schmidt-Rottluff, 20th Century German Expressionist. Additional consideration may be given to the silk screen prints of Ben Shahn and Stuart Davis; also, to the work of Leonard Baskin, Antonio Frasconi and numerous other outstanding craftsmen of the Twentieth Century.

A study of this kind will emphasize for the student the strong contrast in style of the old masters with the twentieth century innovators; the excitement and explosive character of present day graphics activity; the simplicity or complexity of this interesting form of expression. Point out the apparently unlimited subject matter, the wide range of interpretation, the personal quality reflected in the works of different artists, the integrity of materials, the influence of process on design.

Christ Crucified Between the Two Thieves, Rembrandt, 17th C. Dutch, Etching. The Metropolitan Museum of Art, gift of Felix M. Warburg and his family, 1941.

Christ on the Cross, Paul Gauguin, 19th C. French, Woodcut. The Metropolitan Museum of Art, Dick Fund, 1929.

68

Two Women, Ernst Barlach, 20th C. German, Lithograph. The Baltimore Museum of Art, Blanche Adler Purchase Fund.

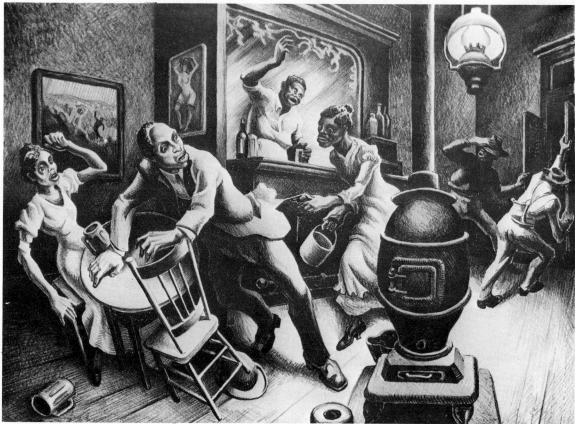

Frankie and Johnny, Thomas Benton, 20th C. American, Lithograph. The Baltimore Museum of Art, Blanche Adler Purchase Fund.

70   *Fish Market, Antonio Frasconi, 20th C. American, Color Woodcut. The Baltimore Museum of Art, Gift of Weyhe Gallery.*

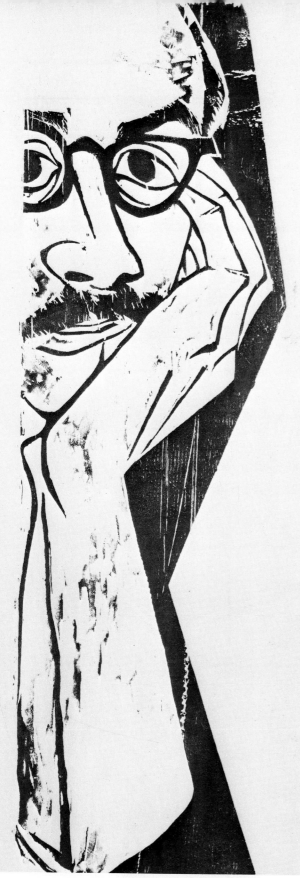

Football, Leonard Baskin, 20th C. American, Woodcut. The Baltimore Museum of Art, Gift of the National Broadcasting Company.

Self Portrait, Antonio Frasconi, 20th C. American, Woodcut. The Baltimore Museum of Art.

The Parents, Kathe Kollwitz, 20th C. German, Woodcut. The Baltimore Museum of Art, Blanche Adler Purchase Fund.

Dancing Virgins, John Blair Mitchell, 20th C. American,
Inkless Intaglio.

The Intricate Owl, John Blair Mitchell, 20th C. American,
Metal Collage Print.

Daasdorf, Lyonel Feininger, 20th C. American, Woodcut.
The Baltimore Museum of Art.

Portrait Head, Karl Schmidt-Rottluff, 20th C. German,
Woodcut. The Baltimore Museum of Art.

The four basic processes for making a print are:

Relief Printing from raised surfaces.

Intaglio Printing from recessed areas.

Planography (Lithography) Printing from a flat surface.

Serigraphy Printing through a surface.

The extent to which a student may become technically involved in printmaking depends, of course, on the availability of necessary tools and equipment and the goals of a particular program. However, the quality of the print and the depth of student satisfaction are not dependent upon the complexity of technique or process. While some methods of printmaking, such as etching and engraving, may require expensive equipment and materials, there are many simpler techniques and materials available for varied experiences in this form of visual expression. As a matter of fact, almost any material, inked and pressed against a piece of paper will produce an image. Then, too, there are suitable commercial substitutes for traditional materials that may be used to help the student to understand the differences between the major printing processes.

Printmaking problems should provide opportunities for students to explore materials and to discover unusual relationships of line, shape, color, and texture. Invention and imagination should be encouraged whether the student is confronted with cutting into the surface of wood, linoleum, plastic, or plaster, building up on glass with fast-drying cement, pressuring a piece of paper against a sheet of inked styrofoam, blocking out a design on stretched silk, or running a brayer charged with ink over a sheet of paper.

Drypoint Etching, Philadelphia public schools, Pennsylvania.

Woodcut, Lutheran High School, Los Angeles, California.

Serigraph, Lutheran High School, Los Angeles, California.

Monoprint, Baltimore City public schools, Maryland.

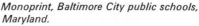

Woodcut, Baltimore City public schools, Maryland.

IDEA, DESIGN, PROCESS

The simplification of the printmaking craft to methods that require little in the way of special tools and equipment has brought this exciting activity into the school art program at all grade levels. The vegetable and the stick have acquired new meaning as a basis for forming printing stamps in the lower grades. Old inner tubes, cardboard, small boxes, string, glue, wax, plasticine, beans, and countless found objects (paper clips, corks, spools, washers, cardboard tubes, etc.) have become accepted as printmaking materials in challenging the imagination of students at all grade levels. The investigation of the more conventional and complex printmaking techniques has been reserved as a rule for the more mature students in junior and senior high schools. Yet the excitement that prevails in the stamping of a simple repeat pattern with an inked carrot no doubt equals that of seeing the first proof from a well-prepared screen.

More important than the variety of techniques, processes, and materials available for printmaking is the sincere personal expression of the student. The ability to carve into plaster blocks, to cut stencil film, or to scratch the surface of a potato is not synonymous with quality in the print. The student must have something to say along with an understanding of the characteristics of the printmaking method he selects to transform his idea into visual reality.

A knowledge of design organization is as significant to success in printmaking as it is in any other form of art expression. The relationship of a design to the potential and limitations of a specific printmaking process or material is equally important. From this it may be concluded that the design and the process are inseparably united. The print should reflect the process and the process must be suitable for the goals of the student.

The developing of a print is at once a total involvement of the student in determining "what" he is to print and "how" it is to be printed. How can the student be guided so that in his preliminary thinking his choice of subject matter is compatible with the process to be used? Or, conversely, so that the process he selects will be capable of transmitting his interpretation into visual form? A significant force in orienting students toward printmaking problems is exposure to outstanding examples of prints as well as techniques and processes through available reproductions, films, film strips, museum trips and forays into the community. Local department stores and decorators ordinarily have samples of textile and wallpaper designs that may be obtained upon request. Other sources would include art magazines and trade journals that place a particular emphasis on this aspect of design.

In addition to this, provide the students the opportunity to investigate the printmaking materials and processes that they will be using. What problems exist in the cutting of wood that differ from cutting into plaster? Linoleum? How may materials and processes be combined to produce other effects? How do the condition or characteristics of the paper (wet, dry, textured, smooth, white, colors) affect the print? An exploration such as this will serve the student immeasurably as he plans his design.

Printmaking experiences ordinarily fall into two basic categories:

The self-contained print or the fine print which is more closely aligned to drawing and painting experiences.

Emphasize:
> The print as a means of personal expression, growing out of the student's experiences, feelings, emotions.
> The boundless source of subject matter through personal observation and imagination.
> The importance of visual order.
>> Singleness of idea.
>> Center of interest.
>> Selectivity in respect to subject matter.
>> Unity of design elements.

Suggestions relevant to developing an idea and visual organization, presented in the chapter dealing with drawing and painting, have application here.

Woodcuts, Baltimore City public schools, Maryland.

76

Two-color woodcut, Philadelphia public schools, Pennsylvania.

Woodcuts, Baltimore City public schools, Maryland.

77

The repeated unit which is more often associated with industrial and commercial design.

Emphasize:

Continuity in the pattern of repeat, regular or irregular.

Non-objective design as opposed to naturalistic forms and shapes.

Rhythmic qualities without a specific center of interest.

The relationship of a design to a specific purpose (textiles, wallpaper, wrapping paper).

A common difficulty in this type of design is that the unit to be repeated often lacks interest or is ill-defined. It is suggested that the problem may be defined to limit the student to the use of a basic shape or combinations of basic shapes.

How can interest, freshness, spontaneity of design be achieved? What are the possibilities in creating variety in an all-over pattern when using only basic shapes? Discuss with the student:

Various methods of repetition; interest created through space intervals; regular, irregular, alternating repeat; overlapping to create new shapes.

Treatment of background. Plain, textured, two or more colors.

Modification of basic shape used in repeat. Change in color, value, texture, and size of shape; introduction of a contrasting shape at various intervals; producing contrast by altering the surface quality of one of the shapes in the unit; distorting the shape but retaining its basic characteristics.

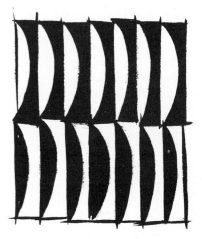

The student should be encouraged to aim for simplicity of design. Preliminary exploration of ideas for repeat patterns may be conducted with cut paper shapes. By first cutting a series of related shapes and positioning them in different ways on background paper the student can try quickly many different combinations. His final determination would then be transferred into a specific print process.

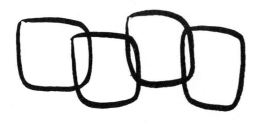

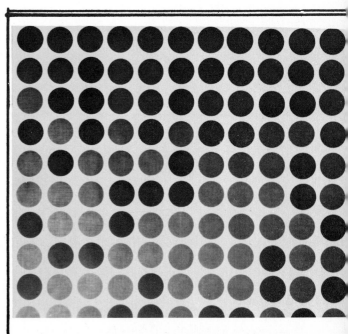

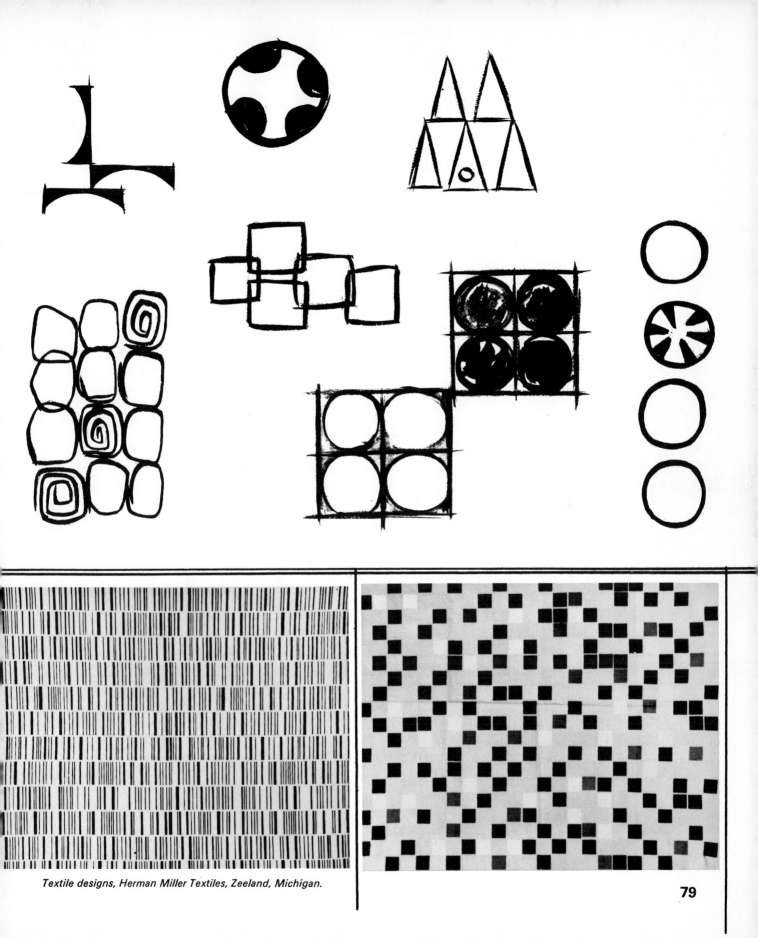

Textile designs, Herman Miller Textiles, Zeeland, Michigan.

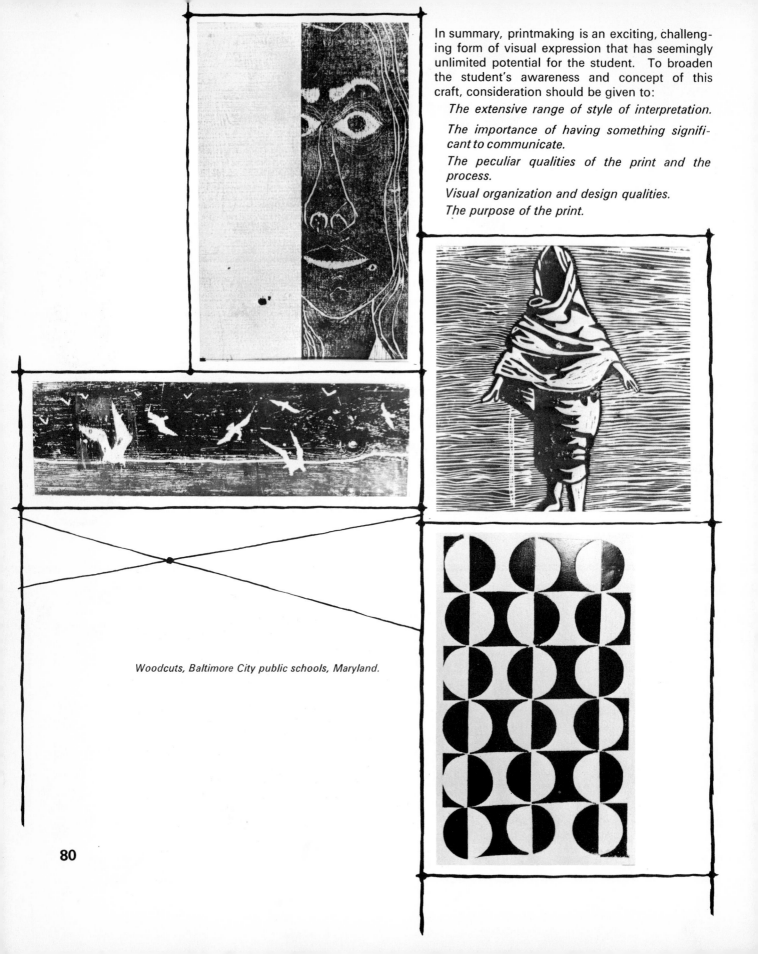

In summary, printmaking is an exciting, challenging form of visual expression that has seemingly unlimited potential for the student. To broaden the student's awareness and concept of this craft, consideration should be given to:

The extensive range of style of interpretation.

The importance of having something significant to communicate.

The peculiar qualities of the print and the process.

Visual organization and design qualities.

The purpose of the print.

Woodcuts, Baltimore City public schools, Maryland.

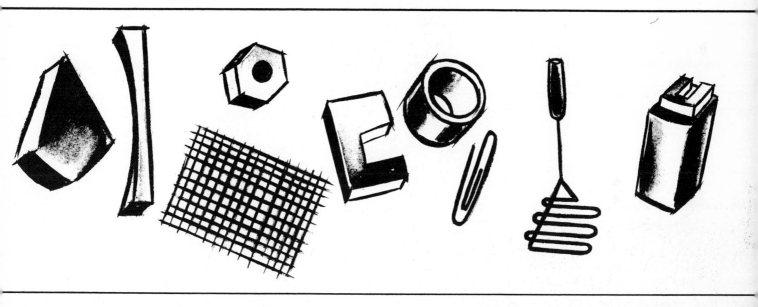

OBJECTS, GADGETS, SCRAPS

Conventional printmaking methods require the preparation of a specific printing surface from which an impression is made. On the other hand some very interesting and imaginative designs may be produced from common items that require little or no modification of surface. Wood scraps, combs, toothpicks, wire mesh, textured materials, string, cardboard, erasers, cross sections of rubber hose, pieces of rubber mats, washers, paper clips, tree bark, kitchen tools (potato masher, forks, spatulas) may play the role of the printer's plate in printing a design. Provide students with the opportunity to explore materials such as these to discover interesting design combinations. To some students this search may mean the creating of a representational design; to others, a non-objective image or an all-over pattern. In any event the spirit of inquiry characteristic of this method of printmaking is usually contagious and the results spontaneous and fascinating.

Preparation for object, gadget, and scrap printing activities is relatively simple. In addition to the items, many of which students themselves will provide, materials may include:

Tempera paint, brushes, paint pans.
Or block printing ink, rollers, inking slabs.
Colored construction paper, newsprint.
The classified ad section of the newspaper and the printed page of old magazines are also excellent surfaces on which these experiments may be conducted.

Discuss:
The repeat of a single object to produce an all-over pattern; rhythm variations between regular and irregular repeat of shapes.
The combination of two or more objects. Certain limitations should be established to avoid the disorder that may result from using a large number of unrelated objects in a single design. Stress simplicity of design.
Overlapping to create new forms.
The use of color to create emphasis, variety, and movement.
Variation in size of shapes for interest.
Negative space produced by space intervals between printed shapes.
Varying textural and linear qualities that may be achieved with different objects.
Harmonious arrangement of line, shape, color.

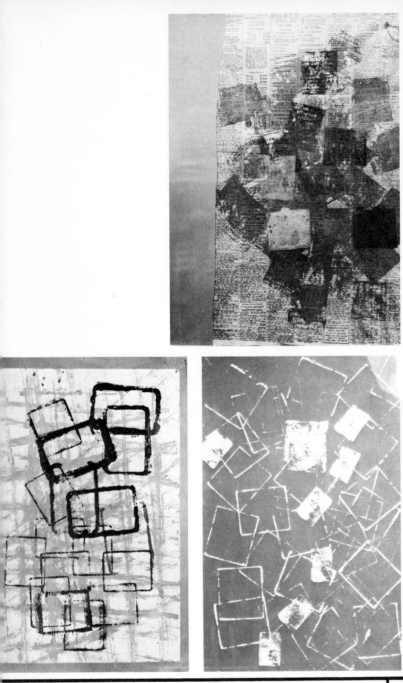

Other suggestions may be made that will broaden the student's investigation of these printmaking materials.

Arrange paper clips or washers or rubber bands on a cardboard shape. Place a sheet of paper over them. Apply ink over the paper with a roller.

Create a design with string by gluing it to a sheet of cardboard. Solid areas may be developed by placing the string close together. When the glue is dry an impression may be made by:

Inking the string with a roller and pressuring a sheet of paper against it.

Placing a sheet of paper over the string and applying ink over the paper with a roller.

This technique may be used to emphasize linear qualities.

Create a design with cardboard shapes of uniform thickness glued into desired position on a sheet of cardboard or masonite. The emphasis in this activity would be on interesting shapes and shape relationships.

Using a roller, create background areas of color on a sheet of paper. Complete the design by overprinting with a found object. The emphasis may be on a regular or irregular repeat pattern. Discuss the space intervals and interest of negative space.

In experimental printmaking activities such as these, students should be encouraged to search out pleasing design relationships based on the nature of the objects being investigated.

Scrap prints, Baltimore City public schools, Maryland.

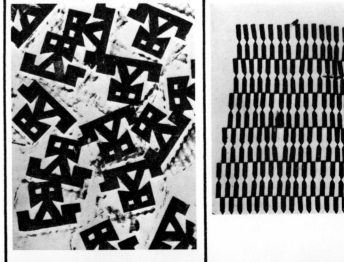

RELIEF PRINTS

The relief process may be described as printing from raised surfaces. The impression is produced from that part of the block's surface that remains after certain areas have been cut away. The print may be positive which would require cutting away areas around lines and shapes that form the design; or negative, cutting lines and shapes into the block; or a combination of both techniques. The resident characteristics of the block (wood, linoleum, plaster) will influence the planning and cutting of the design. The structure of wood, for example, is such that it will not permit the achieving of modulated tones of gray. Thus, it would be futile to attempt to produce a design containing graduated tones of color or value via the woodcut. Not to observe the various peculiarities of different kinds of blocks is a violation of the integrity of the material.

THE LINOLEUM BLOCK

Materials:

　　Inks (water soluble or oil base).
　　Paper of various colors and textures—tracing paper, colored construction paper, bogus paper, colored tissue, rice paper, unprinted news.
　　Synthetic fabrics.
　　Cloth—burlap, cotton, linen, monk's cloth.
　　Linoleum (mounted or unmounted).
　　Cleaning materials, rags, solvents.

Tools:

V-shaped gouge (veiner), U-shaped gouge, stencil knives, cutting board, rollers (brayers), piece of glass, formica, or other non-porous material for inking slab.

Problems:

Prints (representational or abstract), greeting cards, book plates, menu covers, program covers, illustrations (school newspaper or yearbook), repeat designs (textiles, wallpaper, wrapping paper), monograms.

Linoleum block print, Baltimore City public schools, Maryland.

Pulling a proof, Baltimore City public schools, Maryland.

83

84

Linoleum block print, Dade County public schools, Florida.

Development:

Students should be given the opportunity to experiment with veiners, gouges, and stencil knives on scraps of linoleum to get the "feel" of this printmaking method; to discover the potential of linoleum cutting tools for cutting lines and shapes and for producing values and textural qualities. The "discoveries" of this direct search will serve as a guide in the planning of a design to be duplicated by this graphic process.

Discuss:

Preparation of the design

The design may be cut directly into the block or it may be developed first through preliminary sketches. The design selected by the student from his sketches should be drawn on tracing paper to the size of the block.

Transfer of design to linoleum block

The design should be reversed when it is transferred to the block. This is particularly true when lettering is an element in the design. Carbon paper or graphite may be used in the transfer process. A soft lead pencil or chalk rubbed over the obverse side of the paper will also serve for this purpose.

Cutting the block

Remind the students that the surface areas that remain are the ones that will determine the print. A line or the edge of a shape may be outlined with a V-gouge or a stencil knife; the background removed with a U-gouge. Avoid undercutting which weakens the surface that stands. This is most important when it pertains to positive lines. Varying pressure on cutting tools will determine the depth of the cut. Suggest to the students that although they have a pre-determined design drawn on the block they should work with flexibility. The handling of cutting tools may influence some changes that would enhance the original design.

Printing with the block

Block printing ink must be prepared on an inking slab (glass). This is accomplished by placing a generous amount of ink on one end of the slab and rolling it out with a roller (brayer) to a thin consistency. This action will cover the roller with ink which may then be applied to the block. A print may be "pulled" from a carefully inked block in one of several ways:

Place paper over the inked block and rub with the bowl of a spoon. A clean brayer may be used instead of the spoon.

Place the block over the paper and apply pressure by hand or foot.

Various kinds of small presses.

A variety of printing surfaces should be explored. The texture and color of the paper will influence the results of the print. Various color combinations of ink and paper will produce interesting results. Investigate other techniques for printing the block:

Using a brayer covered with ink, roll shapes over the paper. Print the block over this, using another color or value of the same color.

Surfaces such as burlap, mesh, the rough side of masonite, and the reverse side of unmounted linoleum, when inked, will produce unusual textures as a background for the block print. Apply several colors to a single block and print. Arrange and adhere shapes of colored paper or colored tissue on a sheet of paper and print the block over these shapes.

Print the design on cloth (burlap, muslin, cotton). Textile ink may be used with these materials.

A multi-color print may be produced by cutting a separate block for each color. The procedure is the same as described above with the additional task of separating the colors to be used in making the print. By using a master drawing in color of the proposed print, the design may be transferred so that the blocks will be cut to register accurately in the printing. In making a print of two or more colors, the light colors should be printed first. When using transparent inks, the combination of colors by overlapping will produce additional hues.

Linoleum block print, Dade County public schools, Florida.

Linoleum block print, Baltimore City public schools, Maryland.

Linoleum block print, Vancouver public schools, Washington.

85

THE WOODCUT

The procedure for printmaking described for the linoleum block applies to the woodcut. Pear, apple, beech, mahogany, cherry and other close-grain hardwoods are commonly used by the woodcut artist. Softer woods such as white pine or bass may be easier for earlier investigations of this process. Wood that has weathered, often will give unexpected results. The grain of the wood (in some cases very marked), knots, and even knotholes should be utilized in the design. Tools ordinarily used in preparing a woodcut include small wood chisels, gouges, veiners and cutting knives. At the same time, unlimited textural effects can be produced by hitting areas of the wood surface with the edge of a hammer and other blunt instruments (a length of pipe); making indentations in the wood by hammering screen mesh placed on its surface. Small metal objects, nails, screws, and chunks of metal may be used also for this purpose. Experiment with these techniques as well as the more traditional cutting, chiseling, veining, and gouging.

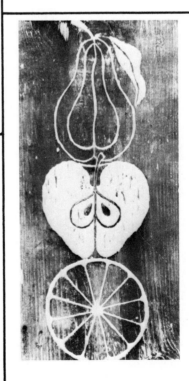

Woodcuts, Baltimore City public schools, Maryland.

Three-color woodcut, Philadelphia public schools, Pennsylvania.

THE PLASTER BLOCK

Making a print from a plaster block is still another type of relief print, the design being formed by carving into the surface and printing from the raised areas that remain. Plaster, because of its softness and porosity, does not lend itself to the sharpness of detail and precise design that may be attained with linoleum or wood. Work for extreme simplicity with an emphasis on shape and line.

Plaster blocks may be made by pouring plaster into shallow boxes to a thickness of approximately one inch. They may also be made in forms constructed out of cardboard strips supported by plasticine on a masonite board. The plaster is mixed by sifting it into a bowl of water and mixing with the hand to a creamy consistency before pouring.

The procedure for developing a plaster block print is similar to that described under linoleum block printing. Large nails, stencil knives, pieces of heavy wire, or pointed sticks may serve as tools in cutting a design into plaster block.

A plaster block, because of its porosity, should be sealed with shellac or P.V.A. to prevent the ink from being absorbed into the plaster.

Modeling clay or wax blocks may be considered for printmaking purposes along with the plaster block method.

THE "3M" BRAND PRINTMAKER'S PLATE*

This is an easy-to-cut, flexible, adhesive-backed 8½" x 11" printing mat approximately ¹⁄₁₆" thick. The adhesive side is protected by a paper liner which is removed when mounting the plate or pieces of the plate to a supporting base of mounting board or masonite.

A design prepared with soft pencil on tracing paper may be transferred to the plate by placing the drawing face down on the plate and rubbing over it with a spoon or a blunt instrument. The design may be tooled with linoleum gouges and veiners or other sharp instruments.

In some designs, the larger elements may be cut out of the plate with scissors, mounted on a baseboard, and details or texture patterns tooled in with gouges.

Non-objective designs may be developed by cutting shapes of various sizes with scissors, arranging them on a supporting base as desired, peeling off the liner and sticking them in place.

This material is quite versatile and economical,

Fabric design, plaster block print, Baltimore City public schools, Maryland.

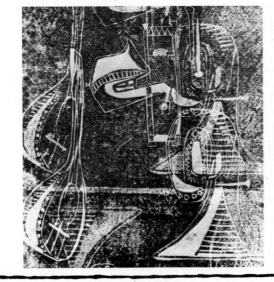

Printmaker's Plate, Baltimore City public schools, Maryland.

88

*Manufactured by Minnesota Mining and Manufacturing Company and available in art stores.

the scraps themselves being of use. Also a design may be modified or a mistake corrected by cutting out the affected area and replacing it with a new piece of printmaker's plate.

The general design and printing procedure described under Linoleum Block printing has application to the use of printmaker's plate.

THE CARDBOARD BLOCK

This technique of relief printing is quite limiting insofar as intricate detail is concerned. However, some very interesting designs based on a variety of shapes may be produced. Therefore, when making a cardboard block for printing, the emphasis should be on shape relationships, variety of size and kind of shape, and varied space intervals between shapes.

Poster board, bookbinder's board, and other kinds of cardboard may be used for the shapes which may be cut with scissors or stencil knives. The entire design should be cut and arranged as desired on a supporting base which may be heavy cardboard or masonite. After a final evaluation of the design and making necessary changes, glue the shapes in place with fast-drying airplane glue. When the glue is dry the plate is ready to print.

THE STYROFOAM BLOCK*

Styrofoam as a printmaking material may be used in several different ways. Shapes may be cut, inked with a roller, and printed to form a repeat pattern. An electric styro cutter knife, or single edge razor blade may be used to cut styrofoam shapes.

Styrofoam blocks resembling the more conventional techniques, may be prepared by burning the design into the styrofoam with an electric wood-burning pencil. Avoid intricate detail and take advantage of the textural qualities inherent in styrofoam. Many of the suggestions described under Linoleum Block Printing apply in the use of styrofoam blocks.

A fascinating print technique that may be considered more appropriately a monoprint is described as follows:

Prepare a design on a sheet of colored construction paper, newsprint, or drawing paper.
Apply an even coat of printing ink to the surface of a sheet of styrofoam with a roller.
Place the design, face up, on the inked styrofoam.
Using a crayon or a blunt pointed instrument, trace over the design. Fingers may be used to rub in broad areas and shading.

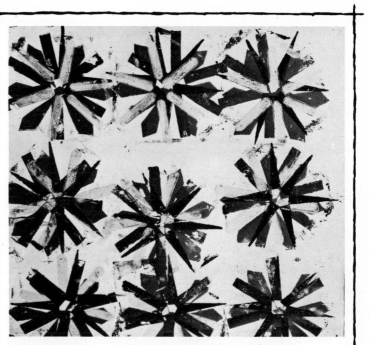

Cardboard block print, Baltimore City public schools, Maryland.

Styrofoam block print, Baltimore City public schools, Maryland.

89

*Styrofoam, Gen-a-lite and the Electric Styro Cutter are available through the Star Band Company, Portsmouth, Virginia.

The pressure applied will pick up the ink, creating the print on the side of the paper that is in contact with the inked styrofoam.

THE GEN-A-LITE BLOCK*

Gen-a-lite is a more resilient material than Styrofoam. It is extremely versatile and all sides of a Gen-a-lite block may be used.

This synthetic material may be cut into blocks for prints or desired shapes for a repeat design with a knife, single-edge razor blade or a heated rigid wire. Designs may be incised into the printing surface with an electric wood-burning pencil or a felt pen. The block may then be inked with a roller and a print produced by pressuring the block against a piece of paper or fabric.

When using Gen-a-lite stress utter simplicity of shapes, bold and vigorous design.

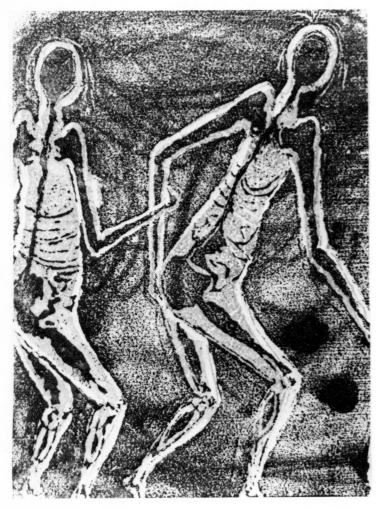

Gen-a-lite block print, Baltimore City public schools, Maryland.

90

BRAYER PRINTS

Producing a print with brayers is an experience that offers students the opportunity to explore design with maximum freedom. No preliminary sketches should be required. Imbued with a spirit of spontaneity, students should work directly on large sheets of paper with brayers of assorted sizes and printing inks of various colors. Students should be encouraged to experiment by:

Overlapping colors.

Placing different textures and shapes under the paper over which brayer is to be rolled.

Combining string with the brayer. String wrapped irregularly around a brayer will produce unusual patterns and add variety to the design.

Using stencils or shapes of paper between the brayer and the paper on which the print is being made.

Substituting cans, cardboard rolls, and other types of cylinders for the brayers.

Cardboard tubes may be modified by cutting various sizes of openings into their surfaces prior to inking and rolling over paper.

STENCIL PRINTS

Paper Stencils

The stencil printing process is a method by which pigment is applied to a surface (paper, wood, cloth) which has been partially blocked out by a design. The desired design may be cut into or from a pigment-resistant paper, preferably stencil paper. It is then placed over the material on which the design is to be printed and the pigment applied.

Several stencils may be prepared to produce a multi-color print. However, the possibilities for using two or more colors with a single stencil should be explored.

Unlike the linoleum block or other relief printing methods, the stencil design is cut as it should appear rather than in reverse. Thus, lettering would be cut as it normally would be read.

The only tools necessary for stencil printing are stencil knives or single edge razor blades to cut the design into the stencil paper; tools used to apply the pigment.

Pigments that may be used are tempera paint, printing ink, textile paints (for printing on cloth), or most any other painting medium.

In general, stencil printing is not suitable for intricately detailed designs on one hand or extremely free-drawn patterns on the other. The hard edge and boldness are characteristic of this printing process. Students should be encouraged to direct their attention to simple design, interesting shapes, and unique color combinations. Additional variety may be achieved in the process of applying the pigment. In making the print, the prepared stencil ordinarily is placed flat against the material being printed. Students should explore different methods for applying the pigment:

With a stencil brush or any stiff bristled brush. Paint may be brushed across the stencil to create a dry-brush effect or it may be painted on solid.

With a spray-gun or airbrush. When using an airbrush the stencil may be held above the material being printed. This will produce soft edges in the design.

With a toothbrush and a piece of wire screen. A toothbrush loaded with paint and rubbed over the wire screen above the stencil will produce a spatter effect. This method should be tried on scrap paper first to get the "feel" of the technique.

With an inked brayer.

The stencil printing process may be used in the printing of all-over patterns for textiles or wrapping paper, greeting cards, program covers, posters and simple illustration.

SILK SCREEN PRINTING (SERIGRAPHY)

Silk screen printing is fundamentally a stencil process. Pigment is forced through a piece of stretched silk, which has been prepared with a design, to the material being printed.

Used in many aspects of industry and commercial advertising, the silk screen print is referred to as a serigraph in the realm of the fine printmaker. Yet the process is essentially the same whether the screen has been designed to print the circuit of a TV set, the colors on a toy, a label on a bottle, a poster, or an abstract design.

Art problems in the school program may include greeting cards, posters, illustrations, program covers, textile designs, wrapping paper patterns and various experimental activities.

Equipment

Printing frame—A rigid wooden frame, made of 2'' x 2'' pine, on which silk may be stretched taut and stapled, is basic. Some commercially prepared frames are grooved so that the silk may be attached by packing the edges into the grooves with lengths of rope. The frame should be approximately two to three inches larger all around than the proposed design.

Stencil print, Florida State University School, Tallahassee, Florida.

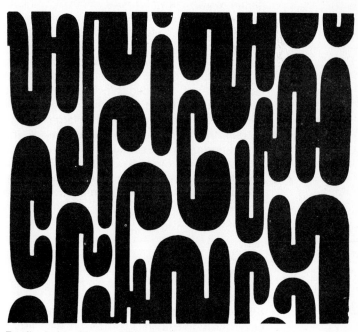

Textile design, Herman Miller Textiles, Zeeland, Michigan.

91

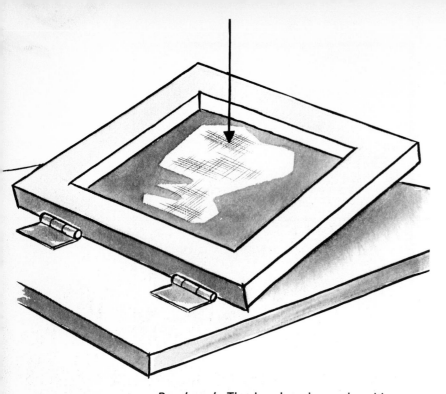

Baseboard—The baseboard may be either an old drawing board or a piece of plywood. It should be several inches larger than the frame to be mounted on it.

Loose-pin hinges—The printing frame should be attached to the baseboard with loose-pin hinges which allow for easy removal. This is particularly important in the printing of a multicolored design, requiring more than one printing frame.

Squeegee—The squeegee, used to push the paint through the screen, is a rubber blade attached to a wooden block. The size is determined by the size of the design to be printed. The squeegee should be large enough to pull the paint across the surface of the screen design in one stroke.

Silk—Although organdy, cotton, nylon and certain net weaves may be used for the screen, silk is recommended for its durability and the higher quality of workmanship that it can produce.

Tools

Scissors, stencil knives, brushes, stapler, steel straight edge.

Materials

Silk screen paints, assorted colors; water-base or oil base. Tempera paint mixed with liquid starch may be used; also, textile colors.

Transparent base; when added to silk screen paint, produces a transparent quality that is effective in over-printing.

Extender base; added to colors to extend them without a marked reduction in intensity.

Stencil film; a film of colored lacquer laminated to a sheet of glassine paper and used in the making of a stencil.

Adhering fluid, used in transferring a stencil film design to the screen.

Removing fluid, used in removing a lacquer stencil from the screen.

Glue (water soluble), tusche, solvents (kerosene or varnaline for cleaning oil base paints from screen), crayons, stencil filler, water tape, masking tape.

Silk screen printing is a fascinating art that has a vast potential in terms of design and technique. A silk screen print may be precise and intricate in detail on one hand or quite free and bold on the other. The process lends itself to carefully planned designs developed from preliminary drawings, as well as direct involvement promoting an exploratory spirit.

A screen may be prepared in one of many different ways. The method of preparation is an influencing factor in the kind of design desired. Characteristic of stencil film is the sharp edge. Crayon or tusche may be used to achieve an irregularity or sketchiness of line. The charm of a silk screen print often may be attributed to accidental passage of the pigment through the design. Many additional resident qualities will be discovered through a broad approach to silk screen printing.

STENCIL FILM PRINTS

Prepare actual size drawings.

Place stencil film over drawing.

Using a stencil knife cut through lacquer part of film and peel off areas to be printed. Ordinarily, a separate stencil is cut for each color in a multi-color design.

Place prepared film stencil under a clean screen.

Apply adhering fluid to a portion of the screen with a small rag. Rub over this briskly with a dry rag. Continue over the entire screen until the film stencil is fully adhered to the silk. Avoid using too much adhering fluid for it will dissolve the lacquer stencil.

After a drying period of fifteen to twenty minutes peel off the glassine backing.

Fill in the open areas around the edge of the stencil with paper tape. Continue with the tape to cover the inside of the wooden frame. The tape may be shellacked to prevent possible leakage of paint in this area.

Attach screen to the baseboard. Place material (paper, cloth) beneath screen and close screen so that it is flat on the surface to be printed. Pour an amount of pigment (silk screen paint, textile paint) at one end of the screen away from the design. Pull the paint over the design with the squeegee and you will have your first print!

PAPER STENCILS

Interesting shapes of paper or specific designs cut into paper may be used in developing a print. This method has more versatility than most other techniques since the paper may be moved easily and quickly to achieve unusual effects. Water-base paints are recommended since they allow for more rapid change of color. When using the paper block-out procedure, multi-color prints may be developed with a single screen.

Arrange cut paper shapes on a sheet of paper beneath the screen.

With the screen flat on paper shape design, pour paint at one end.

Pull paint over the screen with squeegee. The paint will adhere the paper shapes to the screen and print the open areas at the same time.

This method of printmaking suggests experimentation and the "building" of a design. Explore shape and color relationships; also, overlapping to produce additional colors and new shapes.

Serigraph, Florida State University School, Tallahassee, Florida.

Serigraph, paper stencils, Baltimore City public schools, Maryland.

93

TUSCHE AND GLUE

Tusche is available in either liquid or pencil form. Therefore, the design may be applied to the silk screen by painting or by drawing. This affords the student the opportunity to explore and to achieve many different kinds of shading and textural effects in his design. Fine, precise lines, as well as bold lines may be painted directly on the screen. Spatter, stipple, and dry-brush techniques may be used. By placing textural materials, such as corrugated board, sandpaper, and burlap, beneath the screen and rubbing over the screen with a lithographic (tusche) pencil, interesting patterns may be developed.

Students may prepare master sketches, place them under a clean silk screen, and trace the design with either liquid tusche or a lithographic pencil or a combination of both. On the other hand, students may work directly on the screen without a prepared drawing.

The tusche and glue method is described as follows:

Using tusche (liquid or pencil) block out the design on a clean silk screen.

Prepare a solution of one part water and one part glue. Cover the entire screen with this solution. Two coats may be desired for better coverage. The screen should be held at an angle during this step.

After the solution of glue has dried wash the screen on both sides with kerosene or varnalene. Those areas where tusche has been applied will wash off leaving the desired design and the screen ready for printing.

Print the design with oil base silk screen paints.

THE BLOCK-OUT METHOD

A design may be transferred to a screen by using a block-out solution (stencil-filler, shellac, lacquer, glue diluted with an equal part of water). This method is simply the blocking out of the non-printing areas. A sketch may be prepared in advance or the students may work directly with the materials.

Students should be encouraged to experiment with dry-brushing, dripping, and stippling as well as with sharp, carefully-drawn edges.

CRAYON

The use of crayon to stop-out a design on a silk screen usually results in an interesting freshness in the design. This is due to the flexibility of the crayon and the unexpected in the printing. Here again students may work directly or with a prepared drawing. The design itself may be drawn with the crayon, producing a negative effect in the print. Or the non-printing areas around the design may be blocked out with the crayon. Water-base paints should be used in the printing.

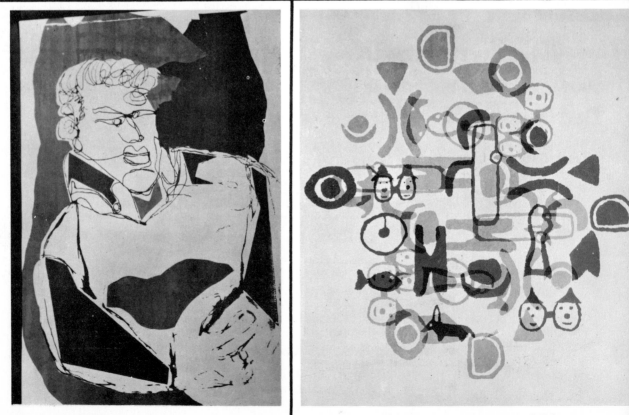

Serigraph, tusche and glue, Baltimore City public schools, Maryland.

Serigraph, Florida State University School, Tallahassee, Florida.

94

MONOPRINTS

The monoprint differs from other processes of printmaking in that the impression is produced from a design or drawing in ink or paint rather than from a plate or screen. It is a valid printmaking technique in that it involves the transfer of the design from one surface to another through the applying of pressure. While a single woodcut is capable of duplicating countless prints, the monoprint method ordinarily authors a single print (thus the name *mono print*).

Spontaneity is characteristic of the monoprint. Yet considerable attention should be given to shape and color relationships and possible linear and textural qualities. The importance of interest in the selection of subject matter and in the development of ideas should be stressed. Students may develop their ideas directly with the materials or they may prepare preliminary drawings.

Students should be provided opportunity to investigate different methods for producing a monoprint. This would involve them in various combinations of materials, some of which are described as follows:

Materials
Acetate or glass sheets, tempera paint, brushes, spray guns, colored construction paper, drawing paper, print papers or fabrics.

A prepared design may be placed beneath the acetate or glass plate. Using tempera paint, transfer the design to the surface of the plate. Upon completion of the painting, spray the entire plate with clear water. Place a sheet of paper over the plate, rub with the hand, and pull the print.

Slow-drying pigments, such as oil paints or block printing inks, may be substituted for tempera. This would eliminate the need for the spray gun. Varying effects may be achieved in relation to the thickness or thinness of the pigment.

Materials
Glass or metal plates, block printing inks, brayers, pointed sticks, toothpicks, cotton, stiff bristle brushes, combs, toothbrushes, colored paper, print paper or fabrics.

Prepare the plate by rolling an even layer of ink over the surface.

The design may be developed by drawing directly on the inked plate with various objects. A pointed stick may be used to create lines; a comb, to show texture. Light tones may be achieved by wiping out areas with a pad of cotton; accents by wiping out the original color and replacing it with another color. Stiff brushes may be used to produce additional effects. After the design has been completed, lay a sheet of paper over the plate, rub with hand, and pull the print.

Another method would be to prepare a drawing on a sheet of paper. Place the drawing, face up, over the inked plate. Trace over the lines on the paper with a pointed stick, crayon, or ballpoint pen. Lift the paper from the plate and the print will appear on the other side.

Other variations may be achieved in the print by developing colored shapes or backgrounds on the print paper before pressuring it against the plate. Water colors, tempera paints, colored chalks, and colored construction paper may be used for this purpose.

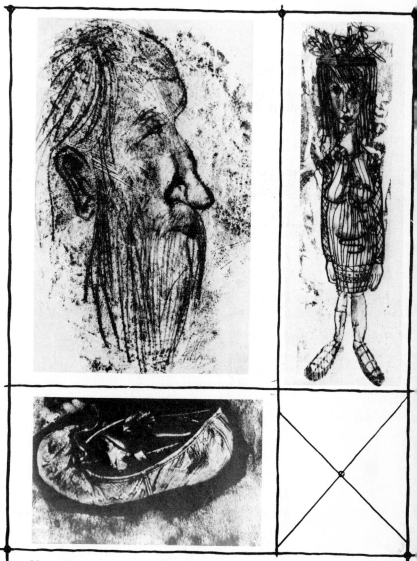

Monoprints, Baltimore City public schools, Maryland.

95

96

Monoprint, Dade County public schools, Florida.

Materials
Glass or metal plates, block printing inks, brayers, stencil paper, stencil knives, print papers or fabrics.

Cover the surface of the glass or metal plate with an even coat of block printing ink.

Place the stencil, made from the design, over the inked plate. Lay a sheet of paper over the stencil, rub with the hand, and pull the print.

Shapes of paper, organized into an interesting pattern, may be arranged on an inked plate to produce a variation on the stencil method.

Materials
Glass plates, Duco cement in tubes, brayers, blockprinting inks, print papers or fabrics.

A plate prepared with Duco cement is a monoprint technique that elicits linear design. Keeping this in mind, have the student plan his design on a piece of drawing paper. Place this design beneath the glass plate. Trace the design on the plate with a tube of Duco cement. When the cement is dry the plate is ready to print. The plate may be inked with a brayer and a print pulled by pressuring a piece of paper against it. Another way to make a print from this type of plate would be to place a piece of paper over the design and roll a brayer, charged with ink, over the paper.

Students may develop designs for a Duco plate by arranging a length or lengths of string on a sheet of paper, creating linear movement and related shapes. They would then place a sheet of glass over the design and proceed as described above.

While glass and sheet metal plates are recommended in the monoprint techniques discussed here, other surfaces may be explored. Oil cloth, formica top tables, masonite, almost any nonporous surface that will hold the pigment being used. More important, however, is the stressing of good design qualities and the attitude of searching and seeking out the potential of the monoprint as a form of expression.

DRYPOINT PRINTS

Materials

Celluloid or acetate plates, etching needles (phonograph needles and similar pointed instruments), etching press, printing inks, print paper.

Drypoint is traditionally done on a metal plate (copper, zinc, aluminum). Tools customarily used include scrapers, burnishers, etching needles, gravers and diamond or ruby pointed instruments.

The drypoint technique differs from etching in that the "biting" action of acid is not used in the making of the plate. However, the drypoint print is produced in very much the same way as in the etching process.

For practical purposes, the drypoint method of making a print can be done quite satisfactorily on celluloid or heavy acetate sheets. As a matter of fact, the transparency of these materials makes it possible for the students to place their drawings (in reverse) beneath the plate and to etch the lines directly over the drawing. The procedure is as follows:

Place prepared drawing (in reverse) beneath a sheet of acetate or celluloid.

Holding the etching needle at a 90° angle, etch the lines of the drawing into the plate. Shading may be achieved through various cross-hatching techniques.

Using a leather-covered dabber or a brayer, ink the plate until it is completely covered. This must be done thoroughly to assure that the ink has been worked into the etched lines.

When the plate is well covered begin the process of wiping. While most of the ink may be wiped from the surface, a thin film of ink remaining will appear as a tone in the print. Care should be taken not to remove any ink from the incised lines. Wiping may be done with a piece of fine-textured net cloth (tarlatan) and the side of the hand.

Run the plate through the roller press with a sheet of dampened paper over its surface. The pressure of the rollers will enable the paper to pull the ink from the incised lines, producing the print. A commercially made synthetic plate is suitable also for the making of a drypoint print. The procedure to follow with this material is similar to that described for the celluloid or acetate drypoint.

While the celluloid or acetate drypoint is a simplified substitute, the students will acquire an understanding of the process with these materials. If conventional materials and tools are available, they should be explored.

Drypoint print, Philadelphia public schools, Pennsylvania.

LIGHT SENSITIVE PAPER PRINTS

Sometimes referred to as the photogram, this print-making technique lends itself to interesting experimentation. This is the only process included in this chapter in which inks or paints are unnecessary.

Blueprint paper, not as light sensitive as most photographic papers, is more practical for classroom purposes. The technique may be described simply as one in which desired areas of a piece of blueprint paper are blocked out and by exposure to the sun or to concentrated artificial light a design is developed on the surface of the paper. The design is "fixed" by immersing the paper (after exposure) in a prepared solution (two tablespoons of bleach to one cup of water). After removing the paper from this solution it should be placed on a stiff board or cardboard and washed with clear water.

Designs may be formed by arranging cardboard shapes, various found objects, paper clips, nails, leaves, twigs, and other similar items on the surface of the blueprint paper prior to exposing it to light.

SUMMARY

The printmaking techniques presented in this chapter should be sufficient to provide students a variety of experiences in this age-old craft. While a diversity of expression may be achieved within the confines of any single method, the study may be broadened to encourage the combining of processes such as linoleum block with silk screen or gadgets with brayer printing. Encourage the students to investigate the tools and materials with which they will be involved. At the same time emphasize the importance of good design and of having something to say.

Additional printmaking processes, including etching, engraving, and lithography, require special equipment, tools, and materials that are not available ordinarily in many school programs. In situations where it is desired to investigate these methods for producing a print, consult books that treat the subject thoroughly. Recommended are:

Printing Today
Heller, Jules, Henry Holt and Co., Inc., New York, 1958.
A very thorough treatment of the four major printmaking processes—Lithography, Relief (woodcuts and wood engravings), Intaglio (etching and engraving), Stencil Process (serigraphy); excellent selection of illustrations showing prints of the past and present; complete discussion of tools, materials, and technical information needed by the student and professional to produce a print.

Prints and How to Make Them
Zaidenberg, Arthur, Harper and Row, New York, 1964.
A well-illustrated treatment of the major printmaking processes with a complete discussion of tools, techniques, materials.

Printing Methods Old and New
Perterdi, Gabor, The MacMillan Co., New York, 1959.
A well-written discussion of traditional printmaking methods and contemporary emphases; excellent illustrations; clearly defined printing procedures and complete presentation of tools and materials for each method.

Additional references on printmaking:

Print Making With a Spoon
Gorbaty, Norman, Reinhold Publishing Corporation, New York, 1960.

Printmaking Activities For the Classroom
Pattemore, Arnel, Davis Publications, Inc., Worcester, Massachusetts, 1966.

Graphic Design: A Creative Approach
Baranski, Matthew, International Textbook Co., Scranton, Pennsylvania, 1960.
An instructive manual of design showing student work and describing how it was produced; presenting a wide variety of graphic processes for all grade levels.

Creative Printmaking: For School and Camp Programs
Andrews, Michael, Prentice Hall, Inc., Englewood Cliffs, New Jersey, 1964.

Printmaking With Monotype
Rasmusen, Henry, Harper and Row, New York, 1964.

Drypoint print, Baltimore City public schools, Maryland.

Woodcut and serigraph combination, Portland public schools, Maine.

Woodcuts, Baltimore City public schools, Maryland.

Rock painting by African Bushmen; courtesy of Frobenius-
Institutes, Germany.

Thirty thousand years ago unnamed artists painted rhythmic, vibrant symbols of animals on the hardened walls and ceilings of caves at Dordogne and Altamira. Craftsmen of primitive tribes fashioned smoothly polished stone implements; decorated weapon handles with incised drawings of familiar animals; produced richly decorated pottery, beautifully proportioned basketry, eloquent ritual masks, and colorful totems; carved crudely expressive but bulbous Venuses. Beginning with these earliest evidences of man's intuitively creative efforts and continuing throughout succeeding centuries, the painter has made amazing record of world events and of people of note. He has been influenced by and made an impact on politics, religion and many other facets of changing societies. He has expressed his personal feelings and reactions on canvas, wood, wet plaster, and paper, with oils, tempera, casein, water colors, chalks. His painting has ranged from meticulously detailed miniatures to huge frescoes on the monuments of architecture. Indeed, the story of mankind is reflected in an astonishing accumulation of art in all of its forms.

Historians have catalogued an infinitely rich treasure of paintings according to the era, the style of major artists, the peculiar characteristics of their works, and specific movements. Often, this classifying has paralleled major societies as they evolved and decayed in the span of time. Painting produced prior to mid-nineteenth century has been classified by various authorities as *traditional*. Representative works in this category extend from the symbolism of ancient cultures to illuminated manuscripts and decorative altar pieces of the Middle Ages, to the Greek influence during the Renaissance, the swirling figures of the Baroque period, the ornamental spirit of Rococo artists, Neo-Classicism with its classical themes and heroic ideals, the human qualities of Romanticism, and the dramatic social comments of Mid-Nineteenth Century Realism.

DRAWING AND PAINTING
Recording Feelings and Ideas

Creation of Adam, Michelangelo; Alinari.

101

The term *Modern* is more commonly applied to painting that followed the initial exhibition of the French Impressionists in 1874. It is significant to note that spirited innovations in style, technique, content, materials, and personal goals of the artist have occurred with greater frequency since this date than in all of the previous centuries of painting.

Progenitors of modern painting, the Impressionists gave impetus to the fundamental concept that the product of the artist is a highly personal thing; that rigid formulae of tradition only serve to inhibit the creativeness of the painter; that the artist alone has the inherent right to determine what he should paint and the form that his painting should take. This premise has been emphasized over and over again in the numerous late Nineteenth Century and Twentieth Century movements which include Post-Impressionism, Cubism, Expressionism, Surrealism, Abstract-Expressionism, "Pop" art, "Op" art, the New Realism, primary structures, systemic painting, and trends yet to come. The classification, Contemporary, tends to be employed to indicate art of the very recent past and present. Thus, contemporary or current art, can be considered as artistic attainments of our specific decade or period.

There are many appropriate books, films, filmstrips, and reproductions available which may be used in studying the history of art. Thus, it is not the intent of this chapter to discuss the chronological aspects of drawing and painting. Rather the purpose here is to suggest ways to achieve a higher quality of accomplishment and greater self-satisfaction in drawing and painting experiences. The examples of artists' work have been selected to emphasize:

> The diversity of style in personal interpretation of subject matter.
> The variety of approaches used in dealing with esthetic form.
> The influence of materials in solving drawing and painting problems.

The Gilder Herman Doomer, Rembrandt van Ryn. The Metropolitan Museum of Art, Bequest of Mrs. H. O. Havemeyer, 1929. The H. O. Havemeyer Collection.

to intense reaction—   *to innovation—*

Conseil de Guerre, Honore Daumier.   The Metropolitan
Museum of Art, Schiff Fund, 1922.

Girl Before a Mirror, 1932, Pablo Picasso.   Collection, The
Museum of Modern Art, New York.   Gift of Mrs. Simon
Guggenheim.

Ondho, 1956–'60, Victor Vasarely. Collection, The Museum of Modern Art, New York. Gift of G. David Thompson.

Drawing and painting, traditionally separated into two different categories of graphic expression, have much in common. Drawing is often described in terms of line, tone, solidity, pencil, crayon, charcoal, and pen, while painting is defined as a process using color in liquid form. Yet, ink is generally considered a drawing material and other so-called painting media can be adapted to drawing techniques. Then, too, drawing techniques may be combined very effectively with painting. Both drawing and painting, although ends in themselves, function in the role of the preliminary sketch for the sculptor, the architect, the commercial artist, the industrial designer, and the craftsman. While certain specific distinctions can be emphasized, the student should be encouraged to explore his capabilities in drawing and painting as satisfying means of personal visual expression. Whether working from observation, from memory, or from imagination, he should understand that his visual organization of elements should support what he is trying to express. His style may range from an intense fidelity to naturalistic detail to an investigation that will produce invented forms, new meanings, and unusual relationships of line, shape, color, value, texture, and space.

Problems in drawing or painting (or any other art form) demand an emotional and intellectual reaction by the student to his environment and to his personal experiences. The nature of his response to a problem is a product of his having something to say and of his enthusiasm for translating his thoughts through materials into visual form. The satisfaction that a student receives through drawing and painting experiences is usually related directly to the confidence that he has in his ability to draw or paint.

105

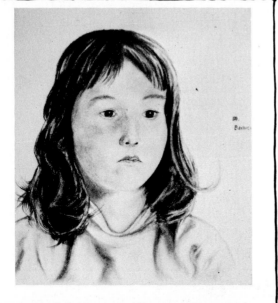

Portrait, pencil, Bridgeport public schools, Connecticut.

Tempera, Bridgeport public schools, Connecticut.

How, then, can a program of drawing and painting be organized to assist the student toward a genuine personal experience?

SUBJECT MATTER UNLIMITED

Consider first the selection of subject matter which is an important factor in the student's reacting to a particular problem. The "what" that he is going to draw or paint is just as much a personal thing as the manner in which he expresses it or the materials that he selects to produce it.

Often an urgency to become involved in activities and materials has minimized the importance of the thought to be communicated. Insufficient attention to content results in a superficial response, floundering, and meaningless "play." Imposed themes, usually confining, dull the student's interest and decrease his enthusiasm for self-expression. Carelessly defined problems ("draw something that happened to you on your recent summer vacation") may make drawing and painting an experience that is little more than reporting (story telling).

What procedures may be used to motivate the student toward a meaningful, yet personal choice of subject-matter? How can subject-matter be approached to bring out the student's interest and enthusiasm for drawing and painting his own ideas, feelings, experiences?

From Caves to Museums

A significant source of inspiration may be found in examples of drawing and painting by artists of the past and present. Reproductions should be selected to show a wide variety of subject matter. This should help establish the fact that ideas for drawing and painting are apparently unlimited. Emphasize that the artist is painting out of his own experiences, expressing his personal feelings and reactions. Discuss what appears to be the thoughts and feelings of the artist as reflected in his painting; treatment of subject matter, personal interpretation, style; the contrasting ways in which artists have dealt with esthetic form, visual organization; the selectivity by the artist of those elements that are essential to a complete visual statement. Follow this discussion by challenging the student to probe his own feelings and experiences preliminary to working with drawing and painting materials.

The Student's World

An effort should be made to cultivate the student's awareness of his surroundings. This is essential to his growing ability to organize his thoughts. Characteristic of the world around the student are the forces of order and disorder evolving from nature or from the influences of man. The more the student is aware of these forces in the community in which he lives the more likely they will

Street scene, watercolor, Baltimore City public schools, Maryland.

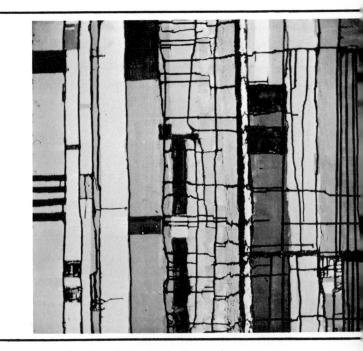

Oil, Bridgeport public schools, Connecticut.

Elegy to the Spanish Republic, 1957–'61, Robert Motherwell.   Collection, The Museum of Modern Art, New York.   **107**

*Christina's World, 1948, Andrew Wyeth.   Collection, The
Museum of Modern Art, New York.*

become a favorable influence in his personal expression. Organized sketching trips in the vicinity of the school as well as other parts of the community will help to intensify the student's recognition of natural and man-made objects around him. Encourage the student to continue this type of investigation in and around his home. Talk about different kinds of houses, patterns of brick, stone, clapboard, shingles; his family or neighbors going to work, coming home, playing, watching TV, doing chores. Discuss the view from the front porch or steps, from a bedroom window. Consider the community, its activity, Saturday afternoon, Sunday morning, a fire, street lights, traffic and route signs, trash containers, the mail box, fire plug, old and new construction, the bus station, neighborhood store, freight yards, factories, skyscrapers, towers, barns, silos. Focus the student's attention on nature, plants, trees, weeds, rocks, a nearby creek. A growing perceptive relationship with his immediate physical surroundings will provide the student with a greater assurance in his drawing and painting efforts. Over a period of time he will acquire a storehouse of ideas and a personal acquaintance with many interesting things that were formerly passed unnoticed. This new awareness of the community and the accompanying sharpening of the senses cannot be over-emphasized as sig-

nificant factors in developing the student's interest and abilities in creative visual expression. This emphasis on the community as an important source for student drawing and painting experiences may be extended through discussion of the works of American artists, such as, John Sloan, John Stewart Curry, Thomas Benton, Charles Burchfield, Edwin Hopper, Andrew Wyeth, and others.

Students sketching, Northeast High School, Kansas City public schools, Missouri.

Watercolor, Baltimore City public schools, Maryland.

109

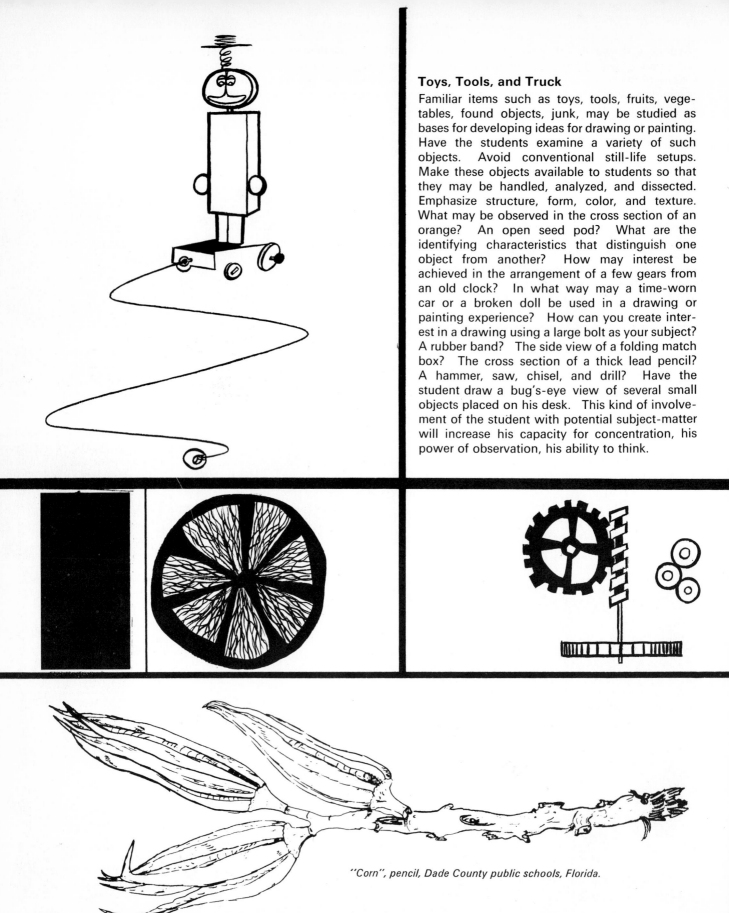

Toys, Tools, and Truck

Familiar items such as toys, tools, fruits, vegetables, found objects, junk, may be studied as bases for developing ideas for drawing or painting. Have the students examine a variety of such objects. Avoid conventional still-life setups. Make these objects available to students so that they may be handled, analyzed, and dissected. Emphasize structure, form, color, and texture. What may be observed in the cross section of an orange? An open seed pod? What are the identifying characteristics that distinguish one object from another? How may interest be achieved in the arrangement of a few gears from an old clock? In what way may a time-worn car or a broken doll be used in a drawing or painting experience? How can you create interest in a drawing using a large bolt as your subject? A rubber band? The side view of a folding match box? The cross section of a thick lead pencil? A hammer, saw, chisel, and drill? Have the student draw a bug's-eye view of several small objects placed on his desk. This kind of involvement of the student with potential subject-matter will increase his capacity for concentration, his power of observation, his ability to think.

"Corn", pencil, Dade County public schools, Florida.

110

Emotions

Motivate the student toward emotional reactions to situations. How does it feel to be trapped in an elevator? Paint your way out of a deep hole! Draw yourself going in three different directions at the same time. Paint yourself walking down the street which suddenly becomes nothing. How does it feel to be home alone on a stormy night? To be lost on a strange, dark street? To inherit a mysterious, golden key? To ride a roller-coaster? Draw the point of no return.

The Unexpected

It is characteristic of the student to accept the known, that which he clearly understands; to look at things from a "normal" viewpoint; even to anticipate the expected in an art problem. At the same time, an essential quality of personal visual expression is its uniqueness. One way in which this quality may be fostered is through visual brainstorming. A student can become quite fascinated with problems that probe his mind and inspire the unusual. Provide drawing and painting experiences that will demand the unexpected. If a ball were thrown up into the air would it come down? Suppose it doesn't! What reaction would this bring? What other potential would the journey of this ball have for the painter? Normally when an individual jumps he can be expected to return a short distance from his take-off point. Challenge the student to express visually a jump that defies the law of gravity. Where would this take him? (Over a tree? A house? A city?) Other problems of this type may require the student to draw or paint an unusual use for a brick, an ant's-eye view of a street scene, a good substitute for his head, a set of legs that would enable him to run five times faster or to see over a crowd of people. Certain words lend themselves to this imaginative approach to drawing and painting. Typical problems would require the student to design "AVALANCHE," "CATASTROPHE," "EXHILA-RATION," "INSPIRATION." Following an observation of various animals, challenge the student to invent new animals or interchange parts, such as a lion's head on a giraffe. An extension of this problem would be to have the student draw a giraffe slipping under a low fence, a "horse fly," an elephant skipping rope. Art experiences such as these will increase the imaginative powers of the student and emphasize further the importance of his having something to say in his drawing and painting.

Sounds and Letters

Introduce appropriate music, descriptive phrases, and poetry to assist the student toward a greater depth of expression. Have the student react visually to sounds such as a buzzer, the clatter of stones or marbles in a jar, a gong, burst of a paper bag. Initiate these sounds so that the student will not see the source. (If a tape recorder is available a series of sounds may be pre-recorded.) The use of timely, thought-provoking material will stimulate the student's imagination, enrich his creative experience.

Oil, Scotia-Glenville public schools, New York.

Oil, Scotia-Glenville public schools, New York.

111

People and Animals

High on the student's list of popularity is the drawing of people and animals. (It is amazing that so many students aspire to draw or paint horses in this 20th century space age.) Yet the student probably suffers more in his attempt for "rightness" with these subjects than in all other areas of expression put together. Although an understanding of correct proportions will serve the student well in this respect, the copying or continual reference to figure drawing charts and animal books will result only in the developing of a weak "crutch" for his future efforts. As near as possible maintain a "live" reference point for figure or animal drawing and painting. Using a student as a model, discuss the relationship of eyes, nose, mouth, ears, hair, to the head; the head to the body, length of arms and legs; the extent of movement and bending of arms, hands, fingers, legs. Emphasize changes that take place as the student model shifts weight from one foot to another; when he bends over, sits, stoops, kicks, dances. What happens to the clothing? Provide the students opportunity to draw from the student model. Have different students strike various poses—jumping, running, hopping, throwing, picking, lifting objects, dancing, juggling—while other students make quick action sketches. Emphasize gesture drawing, catching the spirit of the subject with rapid, spontaneous lines and little attention to detail. Encourage the students to work quickly with broad sweeping strokes. They should work on large sheets of paper (newsprint, classified ad section of newspaper, colored papers) with soft chalks, felt pen, large brush and ink or paint, charcoal, crayon. Combinations like white chalk on red paper, black ink on dark blue paper and red paint on orange paper contribute to the excitement of the problem.

Figure and gesture drawings, Dade County public schools, Florida.

Other activities in figure drawing should be considered:

Pose the model and have the students draw the background or negative areas only.

Have the student draw several quick poses of the same model, overlapping them, on a single sheet of paper.

Limit the students to a single line to indicate the outline of the figure (contour drawing).

Have student models pose in various costumes for drawing and painting problems.

Have the students draw or paint the model in imaginary scenes or unusual clothes.

Depending upon student interest this aspect of expression may be expanded to include portraits, self-portraits, caricatures.

Tempera, Baltimore City public schools, Maryland.

Pastel, Baltimore City public schools, Maryland.

Pen and ink, Dade County public schools, Florida.

Gouache, Lutheran High School, Los Angeles, California.

Cartoons, ink techniques with shading screens, Baltimore Junior College, Maryland.

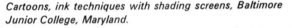

A fascinating outgrowth of figure drawing is cartooning. Discuss the different purposes of the cartoon—political, comic strip, illustrated joke; its role in advertising and book illustration. Emphasize exaggeration, action, simplicity, fitness to purpose, humor. Define problems to include the cartoon figure in appropriate settings in which cartoon techniques, particularly unrestricted exaggeration, is to be applied to houses, trees, automobiles and other supporting elements. Provide problems that will require a sequence with an unusual ending. For example, a three step sequence:

A sleepy-eyed, tattered figure plodding along the street.

Same figure a few steps later with one foot hovering over an open man-hole.

What happens when the figure brings his foot down, unknowingly, into the hole? Think of an unusual as well as humorous ending.

The student will develop his ability to cartoon faces by studying his own facial expressions reflected in a mirror and drawing them in an exaggerated manner. Because of its popular appeal, the cartoon has many uses in the school program promoting health, safety, plays, clubs, athletics.

The drawing of animals should be approached in the same manner as the drawing of figures. Admittedly, it is more difficult to secure live models for classroom purposes, although this can be done in a limited way. One possible substitute for the real thing is the use of available films in which animals play an important part. Sketching trips to zoos and farms are ideal. Good photographs may be studied but should never be copied. Classroom discussions can often bring forth a reasonably good consensus on features and characteristics of certain animals.

Watercolor, Lutheran High School, Los Angeles, California.

Collage, textured materials and glue, Baltimore City public schools, Maryland.

Colored tissue collage, Lutheran High School, California.

115

Summary

In summary, a major factor in the drawing and painting experiences of the student is that he has something meaningful to say. Unless there is sufficient substance to the thought, feeling, or idea to be expressed, it would be better to conserve the materials. A student may be assisted in his personal choice of subject matter.

Through exposure to the works of artists, past and present.

By increasing his awareness of natural and man-made characteristics of the community.

Through his investigation of common objects that have potential as subject matter.

Through problems that engender emotional and imaginative responses.

Through the stimulation of unusual sounds, literature, and music.

By a spontaneous and lively approach to the drawing of figures and animals.

The purpose of this discussion of subject matter has been to emphasize *techniques* for motivating the student toward depth of personal expression. A thorough activation of the student will eliminate the lengthy pause that results only in a misguided drip of paint from a loaded brush as he stares blankly at an empty shape of paper.

Watercolor, Baltimore City public schools, Maryland.

Mixed media, Kansas City public schools, Missouri.

116

FORMING A BASIS FOR VISUAL ORGANIZATION

Whether the student's style of interpretation reflects a deliberate approach to subject matter or a spirit of spontaneity, consideration for organization is another important factor. While it may appear that the controlled manipulation of line, shape, color, value, texture, and space is more substantially the concern of the visual-minded student, this is not true. A sensitivity for design organization plays an equally important role in the expression of the intuitively-motivated student. An awareness of design fundamentals and qualities, in addition to the principles of composition and arrangement, serve the student in saying more effectively what he has to say. If drawing or painting is a means for recording an experience, relating an idea, or expressing a feeling, then there is a definite basis for arranging the structural components of the visual statement, be it representational or non-representational. What should be emphasized in a painting? How can certain parts be subordinated? Is there a single center of interest? Does the drawing or painting say enough? Too much? Nothing? In what ways can movement and direction be achieved? Is it a unified expression? Is the perspective "correct"? Or is it necessary for it to be "correct"?

The student's awareness of design fundamentals and qualities cannot be developed through the memorization of definitions or written descriptions. A sensitivity to these basic principles must grow from within the student. They must become an integral part of the student.

Here again, carefully selected prints, story illustrations, and commercial illustrations may be examined to acquaint the student with the various ways that artists have dealt with esthetic form. Examples used for this purpose should represent a wide assortment of styles and a diversity of subject matter to avoid a limited understanding of the approach used by the artist in solving design problems.

117

Focus the attention of the student on specific design characteristics. For example, the strong, mechanical, arduously calculated linear quality of Mondrian's *Broadway Boogie Woogie* compared with the sketchy but expressive use of line by Matisse in *The Goldfish and Sculpture;* the spontaneously applied color in Kandinsky's *Composition (4)* contrasted with the studied control of color in Leger's *Three Women* and the dynamic organization of basic form and pure color by Malevich.

While it is suggested here that in the process of examining the works of artists a particular element may be singled out for study, it should be emphasized that the "wholeness" or full meaning of any work of art is realized only when the various visual elements are brought together and considered as a total experience. In this way the student will become aware of the diverse characteristics of a single element and at the same time become cognizant of the tremendous interplay of line, shape, color, value, texture, and space. He will learn of the various principles that guide the artist in his arrangement of these visual elements.

To make this search through the work of artists more meaningful, provide the student opportunity to conduct parallel experiments with drawing and painting materials. This will strengthen his growing concept of visual organization.

Broadway Boogie Woogie, 1942–'43, Piet Mondrian. Collection, The Museum of Modern Art, New York.

Goldfish and Sculpture, 1911, Henri Matisse. Collection, The Museum of Modern Art, New York. Gift of Mr. and Mrs. John Hay Whitney.

Suprematist Composition: White on White, 1918, Kasimir Malevich. Collection, The Museum of Modern Art, New York.

Composition (4), 1914, Wassily Kandinsky. Collection, The Museum of Modern Art, New York. Mrs. Simon Guggenheim Award.

Three Women, 1921, Fernand Leger. Collection, The Museum of Modern Art. Mrs. Simon Guggenheim Fund.

119

Line

Discuss the diversity of line; thick, thin, straight, curved, sharp, shaggy, light, dark, solid, broken, horizontal, vertical, diagonal; line to create a feeling of strength or weakness, boldness or timidity; the described line as an esthetic element in a drawing or painting; the implied line as a definitive characteristic of a shape or an object; line as a means for indicating values and for creating the illusion of texture. How does the artist utilize line in the interpretation of an idea? Compare the sharp precise line with the nervous, agitated line in relation to the feeling each produces. How is line used to achieve movement and unity? Depth?

Experiments in which the student will experience the influence of various materials and drawing and painting surfaces on the line he makes:

Materials: Pencil, chalk, crayon, felt pen, pen and ink.

Problem: To express action, fast or slow; movement, excitement, calm. To express emotions; anger, humor, joy, fear. To produce the illusion of depth. Explore various types of line that can be made with the suggested materials on dry or wet paper, smooth or rough surfaces.

Materials: Variety of sticks, cardboard pieces, corrugated board, wire, crayon, ink, paint.

Problem: To discover the variety of lines that can be made by using the point or side of sticks, edges of cardboard, wire; to investigate non-conventional line-producing instruments with ink or paint on paper.

Materials: Colored paper, paste, scissors.

Problem: To express linear movement through an organization of colored paper shapes; fast, slow, or interrupted movement from left to right. Another aspect of this experiment may be to establish a point of emphasis somewhere along the line of movement.

120

Brush and ink, Baltimore City public schools, Maryland.

*Zapatistas, 1931, Jose Clemente Orozco.   Collection, The
Museum of Modern Art, New York.*

121

Relational Painting, 1947–48, Fritz Glarner. Collection, The Museum of Modern Art, New York.

Still Life, oils, Bridgeport public schools, Connecticut.

122

Shape and Form

Consider the meaning of shape and form; basic or geometric shapes (square, rectangle, triangle, circle); basic or geometric forms (cube, cylinder, pyramid, sphere, cone); the two-dimensional quality of shape as compared to the three-dimensional characteristics of form (an illusion in drawing and painting); the active quality of free-flowing shapes and forms. Shape can also function as a portion of form with a number of shapes composed to produce a form, either of a two- or three-dimensional nature. Shape and form may elicit emotional responses in the same manner as line. Low, horizontal shapes are restful; tall shapes are up-lifting. Triangular shapes, when low and broad, suggest permanence, solidarity, stability; when inverted, uncertainty and instability. How does the artist create interest through the shape relationships he establishes in a painting? Variety? Unity? Depth? What techniques may be used to develop the illusion of form on a flat plane? What is the relationship between negative space and the positive shapes that produce it? Does this relationship contribute to the unity of the painting?

Experiments with shape:

Materials: Colored paper, paste, scissors.
Problem: Design a shape that is simple, expressive, and meaningful. Avoid superfluous changes of direction in developing the contour of the shape.

Problem: Create a shape, derived from a basic shape, to be repeated nine times within a pre-determined space. Emphasize movement, unity, variety. Produce the feeling of depth by changing the size of the shape; by changing the color.

Materials: Tempera paints, poster board, brushes.

Problem: Create a unified design by overlapping a repeated shape to create new shapes. Paint the design, using different values of a single color. (This same problem may be completed also with contrasting colors that would be mixed at the point of overlap.)

Materials: Colored paper, paste, scissors.

Problem: Create a design from a single square of colored paper, approximately 6'' x 6'', using the entire piece of paper. Cut through the paper, separating the parts into a new organization. This experiment may emphasize also the search for interesting positive and negative shape relationships.

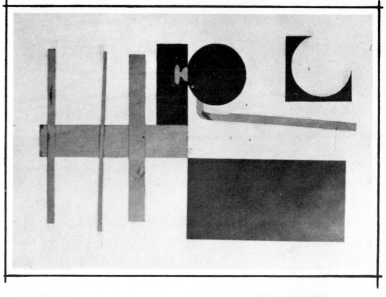

Collage, Philadelphia public schools, Pennsylvania.

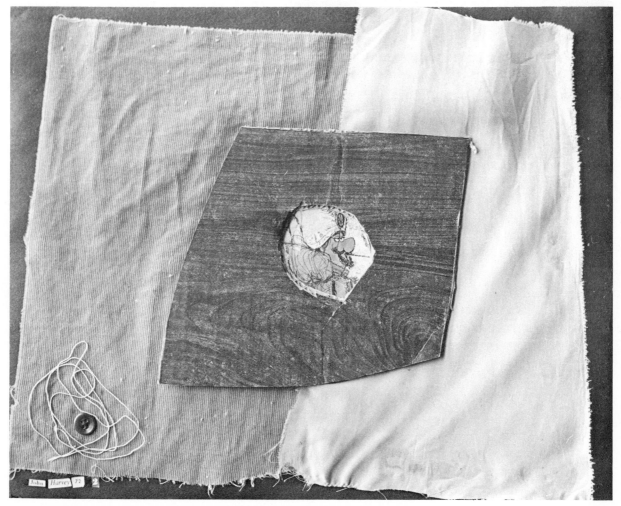

123

Collage, Philadelphia public schools, Pennsylvania.

Painting, 1947, Nicolas de Stael.   Collection, The Museum of Modern Art, New York.   Gift of Mr. and Mrs. Lee A. Ault.

Surface Qualities

Discuss the ways in which the artist achieves various surface effects in drawing and painting; the use of COLOR to express feeling; TEXTURE, actual and represented, to identify surfaces as being smooth, rough, bright, dull, wet, dry; VALUE to show strength or subtlety of contrast.   How does the artist create interest in a drawing or painting through the controlled use of color combinations, textural patterns, and tonal ranges?

COLOR has three fundamental properties:

Hue—the name of the color.

Value—the lightness or darkness of a color. Transparent water colors and inks are made lighter by adding clear water; darker, by adding black.   Tempera paints and oil-base paints are made lighter by adding white; darker, by adding black.

Intensity—the brightness or dullness of a color. Pure colors are at full intensity.   When mixed with opposing colors the intensity is dulled.

Emphasize the effect that one color will have on another when they are adjoining, overlapping, or when one color is surrounded by another. What happens when colors of equal intensity or equal value are placed next to each other?   Discuss the different sensations created in a painting in which opposing colors are used (complementary); in which varying values of a single color are used (monochromatic); in which closely related colors are used (analogous).   How may dominance and subordination be achieved through color in a design?   Point out that some colors suggest warmth, others, coolness.   Warm colors appear to advance, move forward in a painting; cool colors have a tendency to recede.   Also, many colors have universal symbolic connotations.   With the student's expanding concept of color, the importance of investigating color as a personal thing should be underscored.   The artist selects colors that best suit his need.   So should the student.   Color does not have to be dictated by subject matter nor by formulae.   It should emerge from the student's thinking as one force in the visual interpretation of his ideas.

Experiments with color:

Materials: A wide range of colored paper, paste, scissors.

Problem: Using basic shapes experiment with numerous combinations of colors to produce strong contrasts, subtle relationships, vibrating color combinations.   Produce varying effects on a single color by changing the color of the background.

Arrange a series of related shapes on a background to show the role of color in producing movement, emphasis, unity.

Materials: Tempera paints, brushes, heavy paper or illustration board.

Problem: Paint a scene using tones of one color. Paint a scene using the complements of the colors observed.

Create a design based on a single object, repeated six times. Each repeat should overlap some part of the previous one. The paper should be turned at the completion of each repeat so that the object will appear in varying postures. Paint the design using a maximum of three colors. Create a feeling of transparency at the points of overlap.

Still Life, charcoal, Lutheran High School, Los Angeles, California.

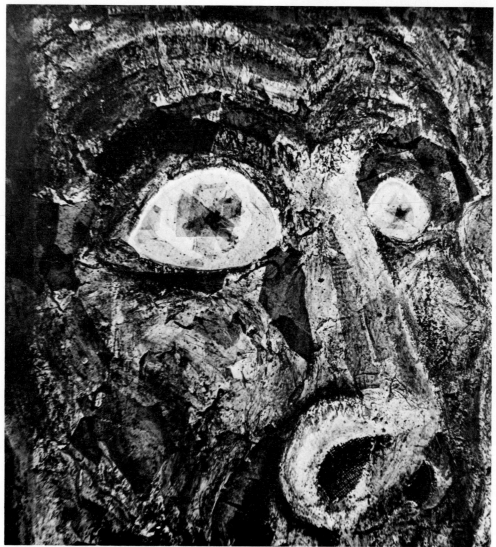

"Head of Christ", polymer tempera, sketcho, and tissue paper, Florida State University School, Tallahassee, Florida.

125

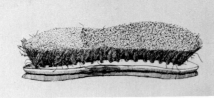

Ink, Baltimore City public schools, Maryland.

TEXTURE, actual or represented, assists in the identification of subject matter in a drawing or painting. Textured patterns create interest through establishing variety and contrast.

Experiment with texture:

Materials: Soft pencil, colored chalks, crayons, paper.

Problem: Explore various textured patterns that may be produced by placing a sheet of paper over a textured surface and rubbing over the paper with pencil, chalk, or crayon. Coarse sandpaper, heavy grained wood, corrugated cardboard, bark, wire or cloth mesh, burlap and other similar materials may be used for this experiment.

Materials: Scraps of varying textures, printing inks, brayers, paper.

Problem: Using different textured materials arrange a design of contrasting shapes. Glue these shapes in position on a piece of masonite or book binder's board. Apply ink to the surface and pull a print.

A related experiment may be explored by inking various textured objects or scraps and inventing textural patterns by stamping.

Materials: Ink, pens, paper.

Problem: Develop a design consisting of six or seven related shapes. Create textured patterns by using various combinations of pen strokes (crosshatching, stippling, variations and combinations).

This experimenting may be extended to include other materials such as brush and ink, felt pen, ball pen.

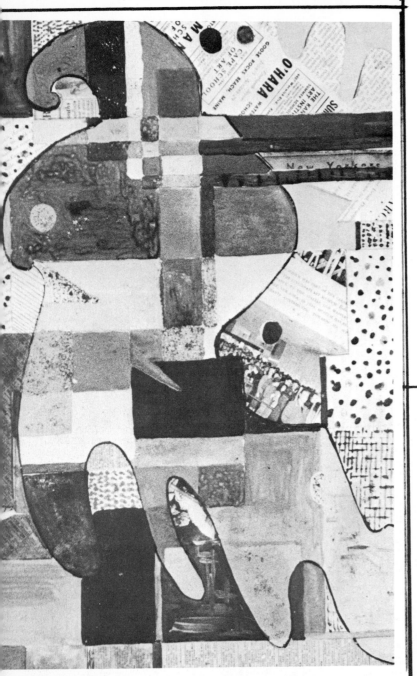

Collage, newspaper, sand, and paint, Bridgeport public schools, Connecticut.

126

Collage, textured materials and glue, Baltimore City public schools, Maryland.

Space

Discuss the significance of space as a major factor in the organization of the component parts of a drawing or painting; the impact of spatial organization on the interpretation of subject matter. What techniques have artists used to move the eye of the observer into the painting? To give the feeling of projection outward from the flat surface? Compare the striking depth of penetration into the picture plane achieved by de Chirico in "The Great Metaphysician" to the rather compact organization of space in Leger's "Three Musicians." How does this contrast with Miro's "Composition" which presents an entirely different feeling of space? Note the converging lines of perspective, the contrasting size relationships, and the changing values in de Chirico's painting; the overlapping figures which confirm the fact that space does exist between the forms, but to a lesser degree, in the painting by Leger. On the other hand, the floating shapes in Miro's "Composition" appear to move forward. There is no concern for literal perspective. Yet a feeling for space is produced by the flat planes brought forward by changing sizes, shapes, colors, and positioning.

Attention should also be called to the negative space in a drawing or painting, that space that surrounds subject matter, objects, or shapes included in the arrangement. How important is the background space, the space intervals created

The Great Metaphysician, 1917, Giorgio de Chirico. Collection, The Museum of Modern Art, New York. The Philip L. Goodwin Collection.

Three Musicians, 1944, Fernand Leger. Collection, The Museum of Modern Art, New York. Mrs. Simon Guggenheim Fund.

Composition, 1933, Joan Miro. Collection, The Museum of Modern Art, Gift of the Advisory Committee.

127

by positioning of the component parts of a painting? What relationship should background space have to the subject matter? How may negative space be used to control the impact of subject matter? Positive and negative space may also be identified in terms of occupied and unoccupied space.

Experiments in the discovery of the importance of spatial organization:

Materials: Felt pens, large sheets of paper.

Problem: Sketch local scenes in which strong perspective is a major concern: looking down the school corridor or from one end of the classroom; looking down a street or sidewalk.

Sketch a group of action figures, having them overlap.

Additional effects may be achieved by using chalks or charcoal to produce contrasting values.

Materials: Pieces of cardboard, ink or paint in trays, paper.

Problem: Dip the edge of a cardboard shape in ink and produce a series of lines on paper to give the illusion of depth, distance.

Make another arrangement of vertical lines of varying weights to produce another type of spatial organization.

Materials: Colored construction paper, paste, scissors.

Problem: Cut several simple, related shapes from various colors of construction paper. Place these on a piece of background paper. Try different arrangements and observe the effect when the shapes are touching, overlapping or set apart. Arrange the shapes to present a progression in the space intervals.

Materials: Black crayon, large sheets of newsprint.

Problem: Represent an arrangement of common objects by drawing the negative space only. (This experiment should focus the attention of the student on the background with no thought for detail on the objects.)

128   *Streetscape, pen and ink, Dade County public schools, Florida.*

Pines and Rocks, 1895–1900, Paul Cezanne. Collection, The Museum of Modern Art, New York. Lillie P. Bliss Collection.

129

Cut paper, Baltimore City public schools, Maryland.

Watercolor, Baltimore City public schools, Maryland.

Ink on colored tissue, Baltimore City public schools, Maryland.

DEVELOPING AN UNDERSTANDING OF THE QUALITIES OF EFFECTIVE VISUAL ORGANIZATION

A desirable goal of experiences in drawing and painting is that the student's work should reflect a unified organization, a sensitive relationship of the components of his expression to each other and to the total form. A contributing factor to the student's satisfaction with drawing and painting experiences is his ability to put together or to order those visual elements that are required by him to express an idea.

The student's plan of action with drawing or painting materials is instituted with the "jelling" of an idea. This may take the form of a preliminary sketch or it may mean direct involvement in responding to a problem. Encourage the student to base his expression on a specific idea, selecting only the essential details as they support what he has to say. All extraneous or non-contributing matter should be deleted at the outset. The student must determine the form that his expression should take. He must select those visual elements that he feels are important to his interpretation. If the student is confronted with painting a street scene, he should consider what impresses him. The activity or movement? The street's shabbiness? The people? A part of a building? A particular building, or a group of structures? Should he be concerned with details or an all-over impression? With shapes or patterns of buildings? With the illusion of depth through sharp perspective or flat planes of color in a stylistic or non-objective manner? Should the colors be naturalistic or arbitrary? Strongly contrasting in hue and value or closely related? Not to be overlooked is the student's selection of materials, the inherent qualities of which play a major influence on his manner of personal expression.

From this it is seen that as the student approaches a drawing or painting problem, he has a complexity of choices to make:

What components are necessary to make his idea complete?

What visual elements contribute most to his personal interpretation?

What spatial organization will be most compatible to his idea?

What materials are most suitable to his intent?

Fundamental to the synthesis of these choices into a successful design, is the student's understanding of those characteristics that are basic to effective composition or arrangement.

Tissue paper collage, Lutheran High School, Los Angeles, California.

Through discussion centered on examples of art of the past and the present, assist the student to a discovery of those qualities that are significant to sensitive visual organization. How have different artists achieved Balance, Unity, Variety, Emphasis, Rhythm, Movement, in their visual expression? In what ways are these qualities employed to assist the artist in the conveying of a single idea? BALANCE is the bringing together of the components or the visual elements of a drawing or painting into such a relationship that to move or eliminate any one part would disturb the entire arrangement.

Formal balance is based on an imaginary central vertical line in a way that one side of the design is the same as the other. In this kind of an arrangement, a unit placed to the right must be repeated in a like position on the opposite side. Sometimes referred to as symmetrical balance, a formal design produces a sense of dignity, restfulness, conservativeness, stability, serenity.

Informal balance is characteristically less obvious. Sometimes called assymmetrical balance, this type of design combines units or elements that differ in size, shape, color, and tone into interesting, spontaneous, moving arrangements. It is the division of space into pleasing, contrasting areas of force. A heavy object near the center on one side of the design may be balanced by a smaller unit positioned farther from the center on the other side. Informal balance creates tensions within a design. This quality may be achieved by combining objects that are unequal in size and contrasting in shape, color, value and texture.

Radial balance is a highly formalized organization in which the design is based on the parts radiating from a central axis. This type of arrangement usually presents a strong circular movement.

131

"Vintage Packard", painting, Florida State University School, Tallahassee, Florida.

UNITY is a quality that is essential to all works of art. It is the "oneness" or "wholeness" of idea as well as the coordination of the parts used to communicate the idea. Without unity the drawing or painting degenerates into a collection of uncorrelated parts. No one element in a design is an entity in itself. Each piece is maneuvered, positioned, and organized to contribute to the harmony of the total design. Unity requires varying emphases so that a design has dominant and subordinate factors. Unity may be achieved by repetition of color, texture, value, shape, line, in a design; by grouping and overlapping visual elements; through the influence of continuity in the background or negative space.

VARIETY is produced through a diversification of the visual elements used in expressing an idea. It is brought about by varying degrees of contrasts and oppositions. Through the sensitive use of contrasting lines, shapes, colors, values, textures, special interest is "built" into the design. Variety in color, for example, may be subtle or quite strong in contrast. Too much variety can be confusing, but a controlled variation assists in the achieving of an intense and vital unity of expression.

EMPHASIS is the placing of suitable importance in various areas of the drawing or painting. It assists in the achieving of a logical order, establishing that which is most important first and subordinating other parts to it. If all of the elements of a drawing or painting were treated with the same degree of emphasis, the design would be monotonous and uninteresting. Thus dominance and subordination (varying degrees of contrast or emphasis), bright against dull, light on dark, large among small, are essential to interest in visual expression.

RHYTHM is achieved through the use of meaningful accents; the organized repetition of visual elements in the interpretation of an idea. Regular repetition, as in a checkerboard, produces a rhythm that is dull and monotonous. Greater interest may be achieved through an irregular repeat. The rhythmic quality of a design may be exciting or dull, fast or slow, obvious or subtle.

MOVEMENT may reflect a rhythmic quality since the eye will follow a repeated movement. It may be described, however, as an established, systematic procedure from one place in the design to another in a sequence determined by the artist. Thus, the observer can be directed through a drawing or painting in the order of importance of its various parts. Movement may be achieved through the use of a described line or an implied line; through the repeated arrangement of line, shape, color, texture, tone; through the orderly positioning of objects; through contrasting positive and negative shapes; through contrasting sizes; through the gradation of colors and values.

Another concern in the student's drawing or painting experience is the space or area in which he develops his ideas, feelings, experiences, or fantasies in visual form. In many art activities, especially drawing and painting, insufficient attention usually is assigned to this relatively important element, which may be referred to as *design space.* As a result, it is not rare to see large quantities of student art produced on the same size paper regardless of theme, medium, technique, or process. Too frequently, it would seem, drawing and painting experiences are confined to 9 x 12, 12 x 18, 16 x 20, or some other standard size of paper. There is no doubt that this unfortunate limitation on creative expression is a product of the standardization of paper sizes for purposes of economy.

The student should be encouraged to determine the design space that will support most effectively his visual statement. He should explore unusual design spaces for his ideas. Ordinarily, the idea to be visualized will suggest appropriate dimensions in which the student will work. This phase of the student's personal expression demands the same consideration as choice of subject matter, organization of visual elements, application of design qualities, and selection of materials.

In addition to deciding on the appropriate design space the student should be provided the opportunity to investigate various kinds of surfaces that are available for his personal visual expression. The textural quality or color of the paper, canvas, cloth or other surfaces on which he draws or paints has a tremendous influence on the mood or feeling that he is able to convey. Ordinarily, a conventional rendering of pen and ink would result in the use of black ink on smooth white illustration board. Suggest pen and ink on blue paper or red or some other color, selected on its ability to add to the completeness of the idea expressed. The student should explore also different textured surfaces that produce varying reactions when brought into contact with the pen and ink.

Still Life, pencil, Bridgeport public schools, Connecticut.

Still Life, crayon, Baltimore City public schools, Maryland.

Still Life, stick and ink, Baltimore City public schools, Maryland.

133

Consider certain modifications of the surface of the design space:

Dampening the paper or part of the paper before applying the medium.

Arranging and pasting shapes of colored paper to the surface of the design space, preliminary to the use of other materials. The shapes may or may not relate directly to the subject matter but should be brought into close harmony with the design organization.

Using resist materials such as rubber cement with water color, crayon with brush and ink, wax and numerous other materials that are not compatible with the medium to be used.

In summary, the shape, size, surface quality and surface modification of the design space for drawing or painting should be determined by the student. In expressing his ideas in visual form, he should investigate unusual design space, varying surface qualities, and appropriate (for him) surface modifications. While this is important in most drawing and painting experiences, the student should be reminded that there are some design problems in which he must observe a pre-determined or prescribed set of measurements. A surface design for a package must conform to the shape and size of the package required for a specific commodity. A magazine layout or a billboard design is confined, ordinarily, to an established size and shape. A mural or a piece of sculpture may be developed for a specific space. In art problems such as these, the dimensions should be included in the definition.

Felt pen on glossy paper, Bridgeport public schools, Connecticut.

Watercolor, Lutheran High School, Los Angeles, California.

134

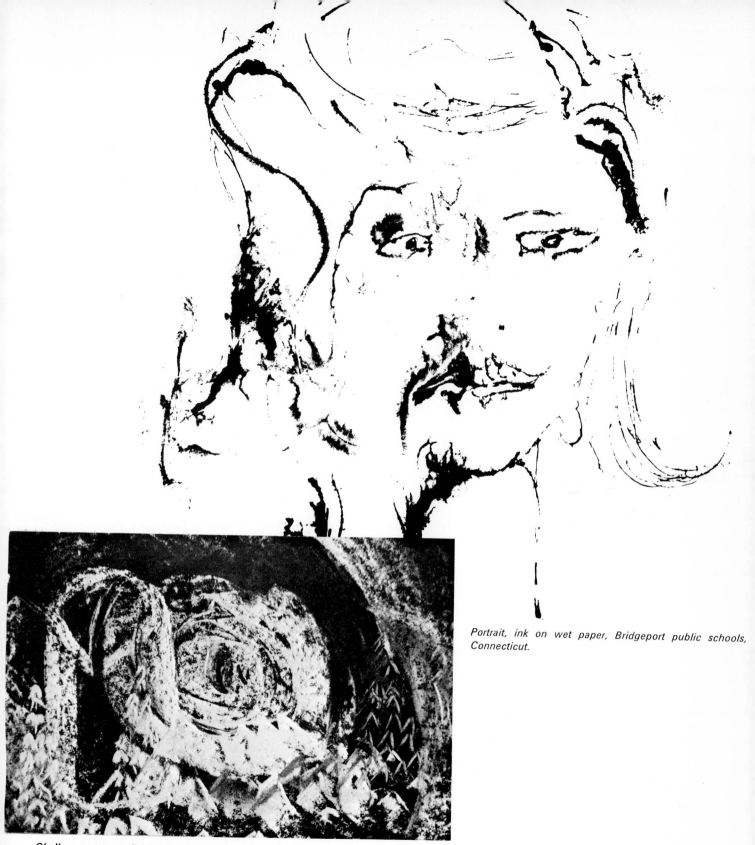

Portrait, ink on wet paper, Bridgeport public schools, Connecticut.

Chalk on wet paper, Bridgeport public schools, Connecticut.

135

THE INFLUENCE OF MATERIALS, TOOLS, AND TECHNIQUES

The inherent characteristics of materials are an integral part of the student's form of expression. The interpreting or visualizing of an idea is influenced by the qualities of the materials used by the student and how the student adapts these qualities to meet his particular need. The decision on choice of materials or combinations of materials for a particular problem in drawing or painting should lie with the student. A growing acquaintance with the potential and limitations of traditional as well as non-traditional materials will assist the student toward selection of materials that are more compatible to his form of expression.

Provision should be made for the student to investigate the various effects that may be achieved with pencil, crayon, pens (various sizes and shapes), felt pens, ball point pens, charcoal, chalks, transparent water colors, opaque water colors, acrylics, oil paints. The student should be encouraged to search out the versatility of a single material.

Crayon may be applied with the point, the flat side, or it may be melted and transferred to a surface with a stick, a knife, a brush. A surface may be built up with multi-colored layers of crayons and scratched into with a pointed instrument. Crayon may be combined with water-base paints or with colored inks as a resist.

Felt pens, ball point pens, various sizes of drawing pens, brush and ink, pencils, charcoal, and crayons are conventional drawing materials. Pens produce many kinds of lines depending on size and shape of the point or nib. Shading may be accomplished by crosshatching, by changing the space intervals of parallel strokes, by stippling, and by spattering. Pen and ink may be combined with water color painting, tissue paper collage, print making and other art activities to sharpen detail or to create a particular emphasis. Brush and ink may be used in a similar way. However, the flexibility of the brush allows a wider variation of weight within a line. Dry brush techniques should be explored (dipping brush in ink and brushing out most of the ink on a piece of scrap paper before using it); also, wash techniques (thinning the ink with water and applying it to the paper, varying tone of value by amount of water). Pencils, charcoal, and crayons may be used to produce effects that are basically similar to pen work. In addition to this, pencil and charcoal strokes may be rubbed with the finger to produce graduated tones, smooth blends.

Drawing materials lend themselves to a wide range of techniques; sharp, hard, precise effects; delicacy of line; nervous, exciting, agitated lines; lines that are uniform in weight or varied in weight. Any of these materials may be used for gesture drawing (capturing the spirit of the subject with many rapidly produced lines), contour drawing (economy of line; single line to indicate contour of subject), or an intensely detailed rendering.

Chalks should be probed by the students as a drawing or painting medium. They may be used on dry paper or wet paper; with the point or on the side. Chalks blend well, yet other tech-niques, such as crosshatching, adapt easily to this material. Chalks may be dipped in water and applied in damp form on dry paper. Students should explore combinations of chalk with inks, water colors, temperas and other media.

Transparent water colors suggest a fresh, spontaneous, bold style of expression; large paper and large brushes. The paints may be used on dry or wet paper, preferably a textured paper. Numerous techniques and combinations should be tried by the student: painting direct with bold strokes; texturing; laying a wash; using resist materials—rubber cement, waxes; scraping into the painting with a knife to bare the paper; combining tempera; blending patterns of color on wet paper and picking out details with pen and ink or brush and ink. Emphasis should be placed on the transparency of the pigment.

Tempera paints are characterized by their nontransparent, opaque nature. They should be applied in a creamy consistency. Students should try different methods of application: mixing colors first and painting; mixing colors on the painting surface; blending, overlapping, sponging, scraping. Tempera may be combined with other media. (Tempera-ink resist: Paint subject or design on heavy board, leaving some of the surface exposed. When tempera is dry, coat the painting with black ink. After this dries, run water over the entire surface. Results will vary, according to the amount of exposure of the painting to water.)

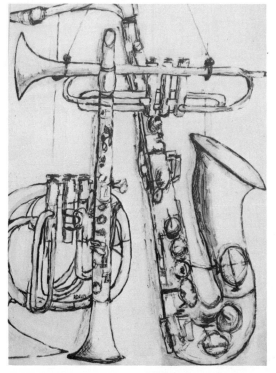

Wash, Lutheran High School, Los Angeles, California.

Still Life, oil crayon, Bridgeport public schools, Connecticut.

Oil paints should be tried on various surfaces: canvas, heavy paper, masonite, wood, parchment paper. Wood, masonite, and canvas surfaces should be coated with gesso (white, acrylic-base house paints are excellent for this purpose). Heavy paper, wallboard, poster board should be sized with a thin coating of glue or shellac. In addition to brushes, students should explore the use of palette knives, sticks, and gadgets in applying oil paints to a surface. Other methods described under water color may also be used.

Acrylics are water-thinned plastic emulsion paints that are extremely versatile. They flow readily from a brush and technique may range from a fine delineation to brushed texture or knifed impasto. Acrylics dry fast and once dry are completely waterproof. They may be used on paper, boards, canvas, acetate, plaster, masonry, and other non-oily surfaces. This medium produces water color and oil painting effects alike.

Collage materials assume an importance that is distinctly different than that relegated to most other media. Not only may they be combined to produce new form, but they retain a measure of their former identity as a scrap of newspaper, magazine ad, photograph, label, textured paper, sandpaper; a piece of cloth, strip of balsa, wood shavings, toothpicks, gadgets, paper clips, string, sawdust, sand, fragments of machinery, junk. The student should study potential collage materials to determine the specific dialogue that he wishes to establish within the collage and the feeling to be conveyed to the observer. An examination of materials will reveal many possibilities for modification to create different qualities. A shape of paper that is formed by cutting produces a contrasting effect to paper that is torn;

Still Life, acrylics, Lutheran High School, Los Angeles, California.

Watercolor, Vancouver public schools, Washington.

Still Life, tempera, Baltimore City public schools, Maryland.

138

cloth may be folded, cut or ripped to form edges of shapes ranging from clean-cut and sharp to raveled or fringed. Balsa wood edges may be splintered by snapping the wood.

Collage materials suggested above would make it possible to create many kinds of textured qualities in the design. Colored tissue used with PVA (or wheat paste) would be relatively flat. Yet colored tissue may be cut, torn, and overlapped to develop new shapes and additional colors.

The combination of cut paper (construction paper) and tempera (brushed, sponged, spattered) has many possibilities in collage design.

Torn paper and paper mosaic techniques are associated with drawing and painting activities. Colored construction paper and areas of color from magazine illustrations lend themselves to this form of expression.

Brayers of various sizes may be used with water-base or oil-base inks, water colors, and tempera for painting activities. Large sheets of paper, canvas and other acceptable painting surfaces are suitable for this technique. Brayer and ink may be combined with chalks, stencils, or surfaces modified with shapes of colored paper. String or yarn wrapped around the brayer will create additional interesting effects.

Collage, Bridgeport public schools, Connecticut.

Still Life, mixed media, Kansas City public schools, Missouri.

139

Ideally, the selection of drawing or painting materials should be your decision as you relate increasing understanding of your characteristics to objectives and goals. Most people are eager to investigate different media for drawing and painting, ranging from pencil and paper to pen and ink, crayon and needle, tempera and ink, paste and paper, and many others. However, since style of expression is highly individual, you may wish to concentrate on one kind of material, process, or method of interpretation.

140   *Collage, Philadelphia public schools, Pennsylvania.*

Broaden the student's personal investigation of materials by including such combinations as:

Sticks and ink or paint (also, nails, pins, paper clips).

An assortment of sticks, dipped in ink will produce a variety of effects that may be utilized in later drawing and painting experiences. The end of the stick may be pointed, notched, or covered with a piece of cloth. A typical problem may limit the student to drawing a figure or an outdoor scene using sticks and black ink on colored paper.

A straw and a pot of ink or paint.

The straw may be used to blow the paint or to drag it across the paper. A variation would be to make half of the paper wet. Place the spot of paint on the dry part of the paper and blow it into the wet part.

Large spot of ink on a sheet of paper.

The spot may be moved over the surface of the paper by tilting the paper in different directions.

Edges of various kinds of cardboard and paint.

Dip cardboard in the paint and apply to surface of paper. Different effects may be achieved by notching the edge of the cardboard. Flat shapes of cardboard may be dipped into paint and pressed against paper, details being added later with pen and ink.

Rubbing.

Rub pencil, crayon, or chalk over paper placed on textured materials (screen mesh, burlap, coarse sandpaper, heavily grained wood).

Dripping.

Paint or ink dripped or spattered on wet or dry paper will produce interesting patterns that may find application in representational or non-objective drawing or painting.

These are but a few of the countless experimental activities to which students should be exposed. Meaningful search will open up new horizons in visual expression for the student. He will discover new linear characteristics, unusual shape formations, exciting color combinations. His knowledge of movement, repetition, and rhythm in addition to other design qualities will reach a higher and more imaginative plane.

An experimental attitude with a variety of drawing and painting materials will increase the student's understanding of the potential of the materials and develop his facility in their use; assist him toward a greater knowledge of the relationship of materials to subject matter. The influence of subject matter on choice of materials should not

be overlooked. An idea expressed with transparent water colors would produce a totally different feeling if it were visualized with pen and ink. A detailed study of a tree may be accomplished better with pen and ink than through the use of acrylics and knife.

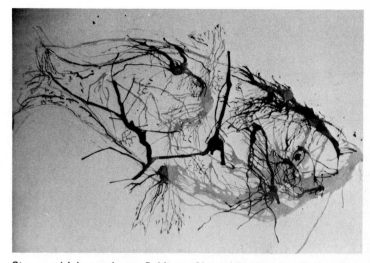

Straw and ink experiment, Baltimore City public schools, Maryland.

Figure, stick and ink, Lutheran High School, Los Angeles, California.

141

A MATURING CONCEPT OF DRAWING AND PAINTING EXPERIENCES

Drawing and painting experiences provide the student the opportunity to react emotionally and intellectually to his feelings, his environment and to his life experiences. Discovering the means to express himself visually with feeling and directness is a personal matter, a self-emerging process. To assist the student toward a higher degree of self-assurance, satisfaction, and quality in his drawing and painting, significant effort should be directed toward increasing his power of observation and developing his sensitivity to all sources of inspiration. This would suggest a thorough involvement of the student; his emotions, his capacity for concentration, and his intellectual understandings.

The student's maturing concept of drawing and painting as a form of personal expression will gain impetus through:

Critical exposure to art of the past and present.
Perceptive study of natural and man-made forms in the community.
Comprehensive understanding of the function of visual elements and the significance of the qualities of esthetic visual organization.
Participation in drawing and painting activities that foster a distinctly personal response.
Continuous self-evaluation.
True search of materials in an effort to discover new meanings for his expression.

These concepts are fundamental to the student's attaining of satisfaction or a feeling of success in recording an experience or an idea through drawing and painting. They should become an integral part of the student as he searches for his own personal style of interpretation.

Drawing and painting activities should encourage a distinctly personal response.

Figure, watercolor, Philadelphia public schools, Pennsylvania.

Ink and tissue collage, Florida State University School, Tallahassee, Florida.

SUGGESTED REFERENCES: DRAWING AND PAINTING

Collage, Personalities, Concepts, Techniques

Janis, Harriet and Blesh, Rudi; Chilton Co., Philadelphia and New York, 1962
The complete, colorful history of collage's personalities, concepts, and skills from 1911 to 1961; lavishly and completely illustrated; vividly presents Modernism's important personalities from the Cubists to Ernst, Schwitters, Arp, Miro, Duchamp and on to Burri, Dubuffet, de Kooning, Kline, Rauschenberg and scores of others.

A Concise History of Modern Painting

Read, Herbert; Frederick A. Praeger, New York, 1959.
Considers influence of Cezanne on the development of painting; a penetrative analysis of various movements which followed Cezanne—Fauves, Cubists, Expressionists, Constructivists, Torchistes, which collectively constitute "modern" art; a coherent, perceptive and enlightening presentation of the whole tenor of modern painting.

Exploring Paint

Petterson, Henry and Gerring, Ray; Reinhold Publishing Corp., New York, 1964.
Presents new materials, techniques, and ideas, emphasizing fundamentals important to painting—color, surface quality, and composition; describes a variety of unusual methods including stick, spatula, cardboard, collage techniques, roller painting, squeegee and sponge painting; resist painting; emphasizes importance of motivating students; includes lists of tools and materials; suggests clean-up procedures.

Mainstreams of Modern Art

Canaday, John; Holt, Rinehart, & Winston, New York, 1961.
Sets the art of the 19th and 20th Centuries in Europe and America against a backdrop of all art; presents literary and social origins and manifestations of the general movements of Classicism, Romanticism, and Realism; although emphasis is on painting, some discussion of sculpture and architecture is included.

Design, Sources and Resources

Ballinger, Louise B. and Vroman, Thomas F.; Reinhold Publishing Corp., 1965.

Form, Space, and Vision

Collier, Graham; Prentice Hall, Inc., Englewood Cliffs, 1963.

Sketching With the Felt-tip Pen

Pitz, Henry C.; Studio Publications, Inc., New York, 1959.

Cartooning

Horn, George F.; Davis Publications, Inc., Worcester, Mass., 1965.

Art: Search and Self-Discovery

Schinneller, James A.; International Textbook Co., 1963.

Magazine advertisement; courtesy MacManus, John, and Adams, New York.

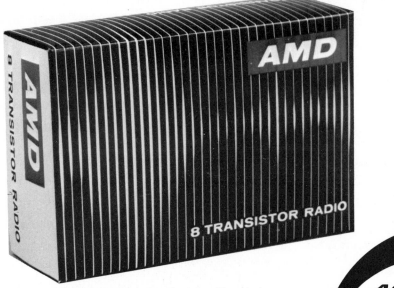

Package; courtesy Art Direction Magazine, New York.

Corporate symbol; courtesy American Airlines, New York.

Commercial art is, in a sense, a product of the Industrial Revolution. While it is true that there is evidence that posters announced Coliseum events in ancient Rome and that a signboard shaped like two large keys identified the Olde Cross Keyes Free House in Swansea, Wales 100 years before Columbus sailed for America, commercial art is by and large the handmaiden of mass production resulting from keen competition among manufacturers. The growing importance of the commercial designer paralleled the growth of industry and the increasing demands of the public for commodities.

While the industrial designer is an integral part of the manufacturing process, it is the task of the commercial designer to project a favorable image of the resulting product. To function well he must know the product, its use and purpose. At the same time he must keep his finger on the pulse of the public. He must determine the likes and dislikes of the consumer so that the graphic image he creates will appeal to a specific market. The commercial artist must be aware of the latest methods and materials that are essential to the graphic design process. He must have the ability to create line, shape, color, and textural combinations that have emotional appeal.

The influence of the commercial designer is ever-present in the home, the community, the nation, the world. It may be observed in a label on a jar of instant coffee, a commercial flashing across the television tube, a package containing a walking, talking, laughing, crying doll for a child. Witness the huge billboards dotting the borders of the highways or clinging to the wall of a building; the posters attached to the back of a taxi or lining the walls of a subway; the colorful window displays, counter cards and point-of-purchase materials that are as much a part of a retail outlet as the items on sale. The production of newspapers and magazines is substantially supported by the advertisements they carry. The retailer communicates daily with the consumer through many forms of direct-by-mail designs—folders, leaflets, brochures, booklets, catalogs. Truly, the product of the commercial designer is a way of life communicating its distinct message in all facets of urban and rural society. It is a tremendous force, and when approached in creative terms can exert significant influence on individuals.

COMMERCIAL ART: *Symbols of the market*

Poster; courtesy Italian Tourist Information Office, New York.

145

1—Cover design; courtesy Adler-Schwartz Studio, Baltimore, Maryland.

2—Poster; courtesy Italian Tourist Information Office, New York.

3—Album cover; courtesy Adler-Schwartz Studio, Baltimore, Maryland.

In order for the student to perform with some degree of satisfaction he should have an understanding of those skills and procedures that are significant to all forms of commercial art. It is essential that the student's comprehension of these fundamentals be developed, as near as possible, in the context of typical commercial art problems rather than through the time-worn drills. In a classroom analysis of professional examples, the student will discover the importance of lettering to the poster designer; of layout procedures to all commercial design; of type selection and copyfitting to the newspaper and magazine layout artist; of the function of color in advertising art. He will become familiar with the relationship of illustration technique to specific commercial art media; the influence of printing production methods on the preparation of art for advertising purposes. He will develop an awareness of processes and techniques that are characteristic of commercial art.

Such a study of various commercial art forms would reveal to the student the inter-action of the component parts of any single piece of advertising. It would point out that a poster is not merely an attention-getting illustration with the lettering "tacked" on. It is, rather, a design that reflects, among other things, a unified relationship of lettering to illustration. The same principle is true in the design of newspaper ads, packages, program covers, and other types of commercial art. All of the elements (slogans, heading, illustrations, etc.) to be used in a particular design must be considered as a unit to assure a pleasing, unified, orderly relationship.

Through this analytical study the student will discover the value of emphasis and various ways for achieving it in commercial design. While a piece of advertising may be comprised of two, three, or more components only one will be highlighted and the others subordinated to it in varying degrees of importance. In designing a newspaper ad, the illustration may be prepared as the dominant force with the heading and text receiving secondary attention. The commercial artist employs this design technique as a means for leading the eye of the observer to the ad and through the ad in a pre-determined direction.

In addition to strengthening the student's design concept, this study of outstanding examples of commercial art will support the need for developing certain basic skills. Special consideration should be given to:

Lettering.
Layout procedures and color.
Illustration.

Package; courtesy Art Direction Magazine, New York.

147

Corporate symbol; courtesy Lippincott and Margulies, Inc., New York.

Outdoor advertisement; courtesy Adler-Schwartz Studio, Baltimore, Maryland.

Corporate symbol for Farm Credit System; courtesy Lippincott and Margulies, Inc., New York.

Lettering

Lettering is one of the most important skills of the commercial artist. It is an unmistakable essential to him in his preparation of layouts, comprehensives, and art work for reproduction. The student should have some basic understanding of and ability in lettering before he is confronted with problems in poster design, program covers, charts, or any number of other kinds of commercial art activities.

An effective approach to building an understanding of lettering and how it is used is to study present-day advertising materials, particularly travel posters, newspaper advertisements, and containers. From this study the student will discover the significant role that lettering plays in the communicating of an idea in many forms of commercial art.

Emphasize:

The appropriateness of letter style to the idea.

The feeling for an idea, a product, or an event can be conveyed through the style of letter being used. For example, bold Gothic letters will reflect the strength of heavy machinery more appropriately than it will the qualities of a nationally promoted perfume. A delicate flowing script, on the other hand, speaks more clearly for items that have feminine appeal.

The characteristics of different styles of lettering.

Examples used in this discussion should include several different letter styles, such as Gothic, Roman, Script, or other variations. Discuss those specific characteristics that make one style different from the other:

Gothic—Sans serif, no embellishments, simple, one-weight.
Roman—Serifs, thick and thin.
Script—Related to writing, flowing.

Discuss further the relationship of letter style to specific designs and subject matter.

The uniformity of letter construction.

In using a specific letter style, consideration must be given to a uniform structure of the letters. For example, in a Gothic alphabet, the letters are all the same weight and thickness. Thus, in lettering a word or a series of words in this style it is necessary to observe this characteristic throughout. When using a Roman alphabet, all of the thin strokes should be the same weight as well as all of the thick strokes. This principle is true also in some of the quite informal, contemporary letter variations that are so popular today.

The consistency of letter formation.

In general, the interchanging of capital letters with lower case within a single word should be avoided. Also letters that are meant to be vertical should be formed to stand in an upright position. At the same time, italicized letters should maintain the same slant throughout a word or a group of words.

The spacing of letters within a word and between words.

Because of the natural irregularity of letters in any one alphabet, they cannot be spaced mechanically. In the forming of a word, letters must be adjusted to achieve an equal amount of space between each letter in the word. Only an optically spaced word will produce the desired even gray tone. It may be suggested that more space should be allowed automatically between straight-edge letters like the "H" and the "I". An acceptable guide for space between words is to allow the space normally required for an "S" in the alphabet being used. If the letters in a word are being letter-spaced, a proportionate amount of space should be added between words.

The relationship of lettering to the rest of the design.

Lettering must be considered as an integral part of the total design. Otherwise, it will appear as an afterthought and lose its effectiveness. In many examples of commercial art, lettering is used to attract attention and becomes the major factor in the design.

The flexibility of a single alphabet.

Although an extensive knowledge of letter styles is of value to the student, he should become aware of the diversity that may be achieved with a single style of lettering. A word or series of words in a slogan may be lettered with:

Capitals.
Lower case.
Capitals and lower case.
Capitals and small capitals.
Vertical or italic.
Bold or light.
Condensed, normal, extended.

However, after deciding which direction the lettering should take, it should be carried out with consistency. If a word is started with an extended letter, the remaining letters should be done in the same way.

Label design; courtesy Royal Dadmun Associates, Inc., Baltimore, Maryland.

Lettering Problems

In providing the student with experiences that will strengthen his skill in lettering, avoid the copying of lettering charts and other procedures that do not allow for creativeness and imagination. There are many meaningful lettering activities that will give him an opportunity to put into effect those things that he discovered about lettering through an introductory discussion, similar to the one just described.

Lettering problems such as name plates, titles for class project folders (Science, English, History, Mathematics, Art), titles and captions for bulletin boards, and slogans will offer a challenge in simple layout at the same time that they are developing the lettering proficiency of the student. The problem may be extended to include an illustration that will relate.

Problem Definitions

Lettering problems should be defined to establish a framework for student interpretation. Note that in each of these suggested problems, the student is required to make some personal decisions that will influence the appearance of his product.

Using the Gothic alphabet, letter a 3- to 5-word slogan on a 5'' x 24'' strip of poster board.
Letter a sign for the school store, using Gothic capital letters only, on a 12'' x 16'' piece of poster board.
Using the Gothic alphabet, letter a title for the bulletin board. Emphasize the key word or words. The title must be read from a distance of 25 feet.
Letter your name on your art folder. Include a pertinent illustration.

Note: Similar problems may be used to acquaint the student with other styles of letters such as Roman and Script. Lettering books or examples of lettering styles should be available to the student for reference.

Lettering Techniques
CUT PAPER LETTERS
Materials:
Colored construction paper, scissors, poster board, rubber cement or glue.

Cut paper letters are suitable for posters, bulletin boards, chart titles, and signs. A distinct advantage to this technique is that if a student should make a mistake he would have to cut only that letter again. A mistake made when using brush and paint or pen and ink generally means doing the entire job over.

SIMPLE
Legible
APPROPRIATE
ATTRATIVE
Parfum
TRUCK

Demonstrate techniques for cutting letters from paper:

Paper strip method

Cut a strip of paper to the height desired for the letters to be made.

Fold the paper in equal folds, thus establishing the width of the letters.

Cut one letter from each rectangle formed.

The only deviations would be the "M" and the "W" which would require approximately 1½ folds and the "I" which would be cut from a part of one fold.

Emphasize:

Uniformity of weight of letters.

Relationship of size of letters to space where they are to be used.

Flexibility in arrangement of letters.

The letters may be arranged on a straight or curved line or they may be moved up and down and placed at angles to produce the feeling of action.

Influence of color.

Experiment with color combination to develop strong or subtle contrasts; to create emphasis; to reflect the meaning of the words.

PEN LETTERING

Materials:

Lettering pens of various sizes and styles (round, square, oval, chisel point, metal and felt), inks (black and colors), drawing paper, poster board, tag board, classified sections of newspapers.

A variety of sizes and shapes of lettering pens, metal and felt-tip, are available for student use. When the student becomes familiar with these tools and acquires some control over their use, he will find many applications for pen lettering. Captions, titles, and slogans for bulletin boards, charts, folders, science projects, posters, and program covers may be produced effectively through this method of lettering.

Lettering pens give the student a different type of experience than he enjoys with cut paper techniques. Lettering with a pen is a more exacting discipline. The student should be given the

Poster, cut paper technique; Baltimore City public schools, Maryland.

opportunity to explore different kinds of pens to search out their possibilities as well as their limitations. This may be done by having the student experiment with different kinds of pen-strokes (vertical, diagonal, horizontal, curve, S-curve) that will have application to the forming of letters. The classified ad section of the local newspaper, turned side-wise, provides a good surface for such preliminary investigation. The lines indicating column widths would serve as guide lines.

Demonstrate correct way to use lettering pens.

Discuss the differences in weight of stroke in relation to size of pen.

Discuss variations in thickness possible with chisel point pens. Relate this to the Roman alphabet and to thick and thin Script letters.

Emphasize clean-cut, deliberate strokes.

Lettering a poster; Baltimore City public schools, Maryland.

Lettering a sign; Baltimore City public schools, Maryland.

152

These experiments should be followed with lettering problems similar to those suggested earlier. Lettering books or good examples of lettering should be available for student reference.

Emphasize:

Use of guide lines.
Optical spacing.
Accuracy in letter construction.
Uniformity of lettering.
Positioning of words to be lettered.

It is suggested that layout procedure should be discussed with the student when he is confronted with a lettering problem.

Determine what is to be lettered, design and style of letter, and the space it will require.
Draw guide lines lightly.
Space the letters in lightly with a pencil.
Using the appropriate lettering pen, complete the lettering.

BRUSH LETTERING

Materials:

Lettering brushes of various sizes (¼'', ⅜'', ½''), tempera paints, paper, poster board, classified ad section of local newspaper, water, containers, rags.

Perhaps the most widely used approach to lettering is brush and paint. Special lettering brushes, usually referred to as chisel point brushes, are available in many sizes. The size of the lettering is a determining factor in the choice of brush.

Here, too, the student should be given opportunity to discover the possibilities of the brush through practicing strokes that are related to letters (vertical, diagonal, horizontal, curve, S-curve). This investigation may be conducted on the classified ad section of newspapers, the lines indicating column widths being used as guide lines.

Demonstrate the correct use and care of lettering brushes.
Emphasize the importance of preparing the paint to the proper working consistency. If the paint is too thick it will create unnecessary difficulties for the student.
Discuss variations in weight of stroke brought about by varying pressures on the brush.
Emphasize clear-cut, uniform weight of strokes.
Relate strokes to various alphabet styles.

When students proceed from experiments to typical lettering activities, layout procedures similar to those presented under Pen Lettering should be reviewed or clarified.

While the above approach emphasizes single-stroke lettering, attention should be given also to

Poster; courtesy Art Direction Magazine, New York.

the "block-in" method of brush lettering. This is described as follows:

Determine the words to be lettered, size and style of letter to be used, space required.
Draw guide lines.
Space letters in with a pencil.
Working over this, "block-in" each letter accurately.
Using a brush, fill the letters in with paint.
For sharper letters, the ruling pen may be used on the edges before filling in the letters.

CREATIVE LETTERING

Usually thought of as an extremely rigid skill, lettering may be quite creative and challenging to the student's imagination. Contemporary commercial advertising frequently presents a type of lettering that appears to abrogate the basic principles of lettering. Obviously, the use of distortion and calculated irregularity in the letters contained in an ad, serves as an attention-getting device. The visual impact of this off-beat lettering generally carries sufficient weight to offset the reduction in readability. However, it should be added that strong deviations from standard lettering procedures should be confined to special situations.

Materials:
Lettering pens, brushes, inks, tempera paints, colored paper, scissors, paste, poster board.

Problems in expressive, creative, or illustrated lettering may be defined in several ways. Words that evoke visual or emotional responses are interesting.

Fire   Hot   Cold   Sunny   Wood
Love   Clumsy   Cagey   Asleep   Power

The emphasis in this type of problem would be on student interpretation according to his understanding of the meaning of the word.

Other problems may require the students to:

Design a word so that it loses its identity. It may be suggested that letters may be moved out of sequence, reversed, merged, overlapped, varied in size and color.
Design a word, using a different style, size or color for each letter.
Design a slogan (2 or 3 words) so that the arrangement and formation of the letters themselves attract attention.

Paper or poster board cut into various sizes and proportions should be available to the student for these lettering experiences. The shape of the paper itself is often a contributing factor to student responses.

Encourage student invention and originality as well as unusual design.

Cover design; courtesy Time, Inc., New York.

VICENTE PREVIEW NOV 23 5-7 PM / TO DEC 11 1965

Poster by Vicente; courtesy Poster Originals, Limited, New York.

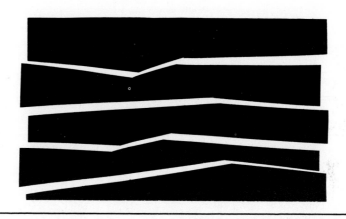

Layout

The layout to the commercial artist is basically the same thing as the floor plan to the architect, the color sketch to the painter, the scale model to the set designer. For the layout serves as a guide in the final preparation of art work for the newspaper ad, the container, the poster, and all other forms of commercial design.

The layout is the visualization of an idea. A most significant aspect of advertising design, the layout is the determining point for selection of letter style and size, illustration, type, color, and the arrangement of those elements around which the design is to be structured. The success or failure of the design centers, to a great degree, on the layout.

It was suggested earlier in this chapter that the most effective preparation of students for commercial design is through the study of good examples of available commercial art (posters, newspaper ads, magazine ads, folders, booklets, packages, and many other forms of commercial art). In this way students will discover the characteristics of layout that are essential to the solution of their own design problems.

Appropriateness of the design to the copy (product, service, event, or information contained in the design). How does the color, the lettering, the type, the illustration, create "feeling"? Reflect the intent of the design?

Uniqueness of the design. Unusual organization in the interpretation of the idea. Visual impact of the design.

Techniques for achieving desired emphasis. Is there a single major emphasis with parts of lesser importance subordinated to this?

Relationship of individual parts of design to each other. Does the design achieve a feeling for unity? Do the component parts appear as a unit? It should be emphasized that no single part in the design should be more important than the total design.

Front and back panels of Burry's package; courtesy Lippincott and Margulies, Inc., New York.

158

THERE ARE MORE BENDIX HYDROVAC® POWER
BRAKES IN USE TODAY THAN ANY OTHER MAKE.
PERFORMANCE HAS BEEN IMPROVED AND PRICE
REDUCED EVER SINCE WE INTRODUCED THE
VACUUM POWER CONCEPT IN 1925. FOR MORE
INFORMATION ON VACUUM POWER BRAKING
WRITE OR CALL US IN SOUTH BEND, INDIANA.

Bendix Products Automotive Division

Magazine advertisement; courtesy MacManus, John, and Adams, New York.

Balance.   The effective use of formal as well as informal balance.

Movement in the design.   Techniques for directing the eye of the observer from one point to another in a systematic, orderly way.

Generous use of open space.   Does the design appear crowded or is there provision for "breathing space"?

Role of line, shape, color, texture, and space in visualizing an idea.

Effectiveness of the design.   Does the design say what it should say in a direct way?   A subtle way?   Is it convincing?   Does it attract attention?

Characteristics that are inherent in specific commercial art forms.   How does the newspaper ad differ from the poster?   The magazine ad, from a brochure?   A container design, from point-of-purchase?

The role of color is of such major significance to layout and commercial design that it should be assigned a particular emphasis at this point.   The examples of commercial art selected for classroom discussion should reflect a variety of uses of color:

Single-color designs.
Two-color designs.
Multi-color designs.

Discuss

Subtle color relationships.
Unusual combinations of color.
Limited use of color.
Impact of color used in full intensity.
How colors relate to each other in the design.
Ways in which color is distributed throughout the design.
Color used to reflect the theme of or information in the design.
Developing of color contrasts.
Symbolic use of color.

In layout problems, the students should be encouraged to experiment with color and to search out the unusual.   Avoid the old cliches.   Through this investigative approach, a spirit of spontaneity and freshness will be engendered.

Booklet cover; courtesy Adler-Schwartz Studio, Baltimore, Maryland.

LAYOUT AND DESIGN PROBLEMS
Materials:

Soft lead pencils, chalks, paints, brushes, inks, tracing paper, drawing paper, colored paper, T-square, triangles, scissors, rubber cement.

Obviously, projects in commercial design should be selected on the basis of the student's increasing understanding of lettering, layout and color. Beginning problems may focus the attention of the student on simple combinations of letters and illustration. Among the more popular commercial art activities are posters, greeting cards, record album covers, program covers, book jackets. Each of these will give the student opportunity to investigate unusual design relationships, to interpret ideas, and to develop additional skill in lettering and illustration.

More advanced problems in commercial design may follow:

Newspaper and magazine advertising.
Direct mail—folders, brochures, booklets.
Containers, labels, bottle crowns.
Point-of-Purchase displays, counter cards.
TV advertising.

Poster; courtesy Egyptian Travel Agency, New York.

160

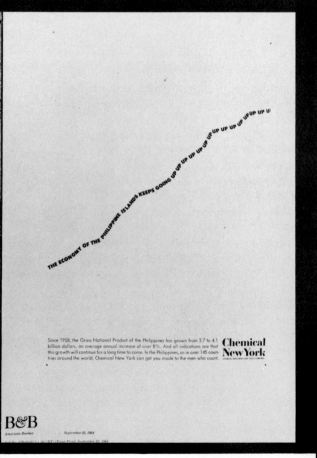

Magazine advertisement; courtesy McManus, John, and Adams, New York.

Book layout.

Story and technical illustration.

In planning commercial art problems for students, consideration may be given to numerous school projects that will provide students practical experience in this area of design.

Posters on health, school plays, athletic events, school clubs, dances.

Yearbook, school magazine, and school newspaper layout and illustration.

Program covers for school plays.

In addition to this, many community organizations offer worthwhile poster and cartoon projects that may be incorporated into the art program. However, contests should be carefully examined to determine their educational value.

PROBLEM DEFINITIONS

Problems in commercial design, whether theoretical or for some specific school use, should be clearly defined so that the student has a tangible basis for his response. The definition should include:

Form of design. Poster, program cover, greeting card, etc.

Topic on which design is to be based. The student must know all of the facts about the topic before he can begin to form his ideas. In a poster design based on a school event this may include the slogan, time, date, place, and admission price.

Size of the completed design. Preliminary sketches must be based on a definite size and shape.

Number of colors to be used.

Materials to be used.

Design problems that are to be reproduced in quantity should be related to the duplicating process that is to be used:

Silk screen.

Linoleum block.

Commercial printing processes.

Letterpress.

Offset lithography.

Emphasize:

The need for researching a design problem to gather as many facts as possible. This will assist the student to a response that will reflect greater depth. The more the student knows about the topic under consideration, the better are the possibilities for his personal visual reaction.

Poster; courtesy Italian Tourist Information Office, New York.

Corporate symbol; courtesy Lippincott and Margulies, Inc., New York.

161

An experimental exploratory spirit. The student's design should bear his signature alone. This can be achieved only by encouraging student investigation of unusual design relationships and by stressing a search with materials, tools, and processes.

The significance of the thumbnail sketch. This is perhaps the most momentous phase of the design process, because it is in the preliminary sketch that the idea is born. Encourage the student to explore many different arrangements of the elements to be used in the design; to experiment with line, shape, color, lettering, illustration, in an effort to achieve the most effective visual organization for a specific problem.

The need for accuracy in thumbnail sketches. The thumbnail sketch, though rough, should be prepared as a miniature of the proposed design. Otherwise, it is of little value.

The role of the comprehensive sketch. The comprehensive is an extension of the thumbnail sketch. The student should select what appears to him to be the best of his series of thumbnail sketches. (An evaluation, either classwide or individual, is most desirable at this stage of the design.) He then should enlarge this to actual size on tracing paper for further examination and evaluation.

Upon the completion of the design procedure described here the student should prepare the final art work on poster board or illustration board. If the design is to be duplicated by silk screen or by linoleum block the comprehensive sketch should be sufficient for preparing the screen or the block. Designs that are to be reproduced by commercial printing techniques require a final drawing, prepared according to the printing process to be used.

Some commercial design problems, particularly posters and program covers, lend themselves to cut paper design techniques. The student should investigate possible solutions first through preliminary sketches. He would then enlarge this idea to actual size using cut paper of the desired colors. This technique is extremely flexible because it provides the student opportunity for further exploration. Lettering and illustration in cut paper form may be moved around in an additional search for the best possible solution before the student pastes them in position.

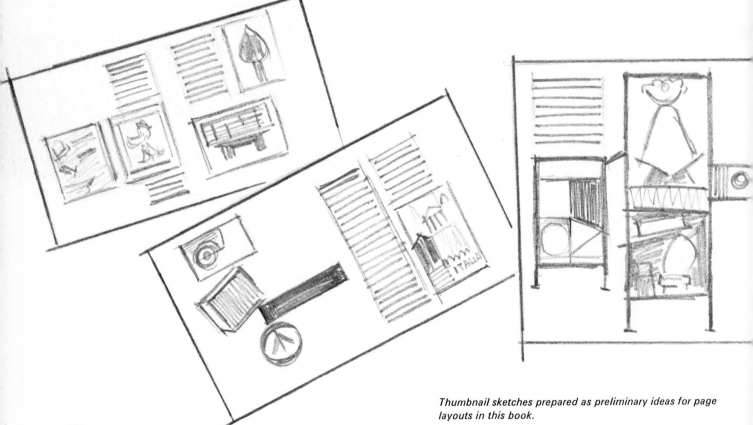

Thumbnail sketches prepared as preliminary ideas for page layouts in this book.

162

Cover design; courtesy Time, Inc., New York.

Illustration, pen and ink, by Jan Balet; courtesy
SEVENTEEN Magazine, New York.

Illustration

An integral part of commercial design is illustration. While an understanding of lettering, layout, and color will help the student in the organizing of the component parts of a particular design, a knowledge of commercial illustration will assist him toward finalizing his design in a more visually effective way.

A diversity of techniques and styles, characteristic of commercial illustration, is reflected in the many forms of commercial design. From pen and ink drawings in newspaper ads to full color illustrations in magazines, there is a tremendous variety in commercial illustration. The commercial artist may be called upon to produce technical illustrations for a trade paper, cartoons for a folder, stylized drawings for a book, a drawing of a hand, a head, a lawnmower, a shoe, an automobile, a can, a space capsule. Every type of illustration possible falls into the realm of the commercial artist.

This area of commercial design is a highly specialized one. It certainly could not be expected that a single artist would be proficient in all aspects of commercial illustration. There are those who specialize in fashion illustration; others, in furniture drawing, or cartooning, or technical illustration, or any one of the numerous areas of commercial illustration.

However, an ability to draw figures, animals, and objects as well as an understanding of pictorial organization and a variety of illustration techniques, will facilitate the student's interpretation of commercial art problems.

Through an investigation of good examples of illustration from all forms of commercial design the student will develop an awareness of the multiplicity of styles and techniques employed by commercial illustrators. Have the students bring in several such examples that may be used in classroom discussion.

Discuss:
   Appropriateness of illustration to content or subject-matter. How does the illustration interpret the story?
   Relationship of illustration to the specific commercial design form. How does an illustration for a poster compare to that of a newspaper ad, a package, a book, a folder?
   The effect of a black and white illustration as compared to one in two colors? Three colors? Full color? How color is used in an illustration as a means for interpreting the idea.
   The many different techniques. Pen and ink, wash, water color, scratchboard, etc. Line

Illustration for a booklet; courtesy Lippincott and Margulies, Inc., New York.

Poster; courtesy Italian Tourist Information Office, New York.

Poster; courtesy Roswell Park Memorial Institute, New York.

Fashion illustration; courtesy Art Direction Magazine, New York.

165

drawings versus halftone drawings.

The relationship of the illustration to the other component parts of the design.

PROBLEMS IN ILLUSTRATION

Materials:

Inks, watercolors, tempera paints, colored paper, brushes, pens, crayons, chalks, pencils, drawing paper, illustration board, rubber cement. When possible, certain materials designed to produce special effects should be made available to the student: scratchboard, coquille board, craftint board, shading screens.

While the students should be encouraged to examine the drawings of commercial illustrators, they should not be allowed to copy this work! They should explore illustration techniques by drawing from objects (toys, tools, handbags, small equipment, books, artroom furniture, and many other readily available items) from memory, or from imagination. The emphasis should be on the development of personal style.

Student activities in commercial illustration may be provided in terms of a specific commercial design problem. This would allow concentration on the characteristics of a single type of illustration. For example, in the design of a poster such things as simplicity of illustration rather than intricate detail would be emphasized. It would also be suggested that the student should work for boldness, and the use of strong color and flat areas. Tempera paint or colored paper or a combination of both may be the recommended materials. An additional part of this problem may be the preparation of an illustration that can be reproduced by the silk screen printing process.

Other illustration problems providing experience in fashion or furniture illustration may be developed in a similar way. Here the emphasis may be on black and white drawings for newspaper advertising. Pen and ink, brush and ink, and wash techniques should be explored for this type of illustration. A wash drawing has characteristics similar to a water color. The major difference is that a wash drawing is completed by using only ivory black or lamp black in various tones. Some reference may be made at this time to pen and ink drawings as being line drawings and wash drawings as halftones. This is of major importance in the reproduction of a drawing by conventional printing processes. A line drawing (pen and ink) is photographed directly in the preparation of a negative used in the making of a printing plate. A halftone (wash drawing) is made by introducing a screen between the drawing and the camera lens when making a negative.

Outdoor advertisement; courtesy Adler-Schwartz Studio, Baltimore, Maryland.

The screen reduces the various tones in a wash drawing to small dots, thus making it possible to produce a plate for printing purposes. A class visit to a local printing firm would serve to clarify this technicality further. Also, an examination of a halftone drawing or a photograph from a newspaper with a magnifying glass will reveal the dot structure of the reproduced illustration.

Additional problems may be presented as follows:

Illustrate a segment of a story. This may be integrated with the English literature program or be based on the student's selection from his personal reading. Children's books also relate well to this problem. Materials: Tempera paints, water colors, or colored inks.

Illustrate a proverb or a motto. Materials: Tempera paint.

Illustrate a humorous line or a joke. This kind of problem will open up the whole area of cartooning and imaginative drawing. Materials: Brush and ink.

Draw a cartoon sequence. Materials: Pen and ink.

Make an illustration for a familiar record. Materials: Tempera paint or colored tissue and P.V.A.

Illustrate a current event. Political cartoons provide opportunity for developing personal style. Materials: Black crayon, brush and ink, pen and ink.

Prepare an illustration for the sports page of the school newspaper; an illustration for the yearbook. Materials: Black crayon, brush and ink, pen and ink.

Discuss:

Realism and accuracy in commercial illustration.

The role of symbolism in commercial illustration.

The possibilities for the cartoon and caricature.

Action, exaggeration.

Stylized drawing.

Appropriateness of illustration to subject-matter. Specific appeal is of major importance. A fine delicate drawing may have feminine appeal but would be a failure when related to heavy machinery, trucks, or items that would ordinarily be of interest to men only.

Unusual color, line, and tone relationship should be explored by the student. A line drawing is not limited to black on white but may be white on black or light blue on deep purple or any number of other combinations. The entry of the observer into an illustration does not always have

BENDIX VARAMATIC® POWER STEERING. THE END PRODUCT OF MORE THAN 27 YEARS OF POWER STEERING DEVELOPMENT. FROM THE TIME WE INTRODUCED THE CONCEPT OF A HYDRAULIC POWER STEERING SYSTEM, TO TODAY'S VARIABLE RATIO GEAR, YOU'LL FIND TOMORROW'S STEERING AT BENDIX TODAY. FOR MORE INFORMATION, WRITE US AT SOUTH BEND, INDIANA.

Bendix Products Automotive Division

Magazine advertisement; courtesy MacManus, John, and Adams, New York.

to be from the normal frontal position but may be from above or below or from an unexpected angle. Challenge the student to be different in his visual interpretation of an idea, for it is that which is different that attracts the attention.

Conclusion

This chapter has attempted to present some of the major concerns of commercial design. The emphasis has been on lettering techniques, simple layout procedures, color, and an approach to illustration. The student, through experiences in these essentials of commercial design, should acquire a greater awareness of the role of advertising art in today's community. Application of these principles to school-related problems (posters, program covers, bulletin boards, yearbooks, school newspapers) should assure a higher quality of student work. These goals should be sufficient for most school art programs.

In special situations where a more intense study of commercial design is required, greater consideration should be given to such commercial design skills and technicalities as:

Use and care of drawing instruments.
Airbrush techniques.
Use of mounting irons.
Typographic layout.
Printing methods (letterpress, gravure, offset lithography).
Imposition of pages in a form.
Page sizes.
Column widths.
Mechanics of packaging.

Many good references are available with detailed explanations of these factors that are a part of the profession of the commercial designer.

SUGGESTED REFERENCES: COMMERCIAL ART

ATA Hand Book
Herold, Don, Advertising Typographers Association of America, Inc., New York, 1956.

Posters
Horn, George F., Davis Publications, Inc., Worcester, Massachusetts, 1964.

Cartooning
Horn, George F., Davis Publications, Inc., Worcester, Massachusetts, 1965.

Graphic Design
Cataldo, John W., International Textbook Co., Scranton, Pa., 1965.

Layout
Ballinger, Raymond A., Reinhold Publishing Co., New York, 1965.

Language of Vision
Kepes, Gyorgy, Paul Theobald Co., Chicago, 1964.

Visual Design in Action—Principles, Purposes
Sutnar, Ladislau, Hastings House, Inc., New York, 1961.

Dynamic Display
Bernard, Frank S., Display World Publishers, Cincinnati, Ohio, 1965.

Type and Lettering
Longyear, William, Viking Press, New York, 1962.

Lettering Art in Modern Use
Ballinger, Raymond A., Reinhold Publishing Corp., New York, 1956.

Illustration, pen and ink, by Jan Balet; courtesy SEVENTEEN Magazine, New York.

Cover design; courtesy Time, Inc., New York.

*Stoneware vase by Charles McKee; courtesy Everson
Museum of Art, Syracuse, New York.*

The product of the craftsman is identified ordinarily as being somewhat different from the work of the artist. This differentiation has been magnified by persisting divergent labels such as artist for painter, craftsman for potter; Fine Arts for painting, sculpture, architecture, printmaking; Applied Arts for weaving, ceramics, jewelry, stitchery, mosaics; Arts for a magnificent frieze adorning the side of a building; Crafts for a carefully incised design on the surface of a beautiful vase.

Unfortunately, this traditional insistence on the separation of the work of the ''artist'' from that of the ''craftsman'' has tended sometimes to relegate the crafts to an undeserved point of prestige more or less lower than the so-called Fine Arts. Yet the only acceptable characteristic that should distinguish the work of the craftsman from that of the artist is the practical connection of utility. While this is indeed an important distinction, the quality of design in a rug, the delicate form of a piece of jewelry, or the brilliant pattern of glazes on a ceramic bowl often lifts the product beyond its utilitarian value.

The earliest evidences of the artistic impulses of man are found in objects that had an obvious functional purpose. Products, mirroring the societies in which they were produced, may be traced back to the masterfully decorated pots, eloquently carved wooden bowls, and skillfully ornamented basketry of primitive tribes. Thus, from the dawn of civilization and continuing until today, man the craftsman has felt the need to unite the esthetic with the functional in his supplying of various societies with useful products.

CRAFTS: *Form and Function*

Jewelry; courtesy America House, New York.

171

With the advent of the Industrial Revolution in the Nineteenth Century, the craftsman was replaced by the machine. Mass production of functional commodities emphasized the usefulness, economy, and efficiency of machine-made products at the expense of esthetic appearance. In a relatively short time, it was recognized that it was not enough for a product just to be useful, but that it had to be beautiful and satisfying to handle. Many attempts were made at first to adapt traditional forms from original pieces of art to the product. Decorations and motifs from ancient civilizations became popularized in the cast iron of wood or coal burning kitchen stoves. Structural elements in power machinery of industry were disguised as Greek columns. Although these efforts to create a kind of beauty that would be suitable to the materials and purposes of the product accomplished little esthetically, they did serve as the springboard for today's industrial designer. The greatest single influence on Twentieth Century product design has been the Bauhaus, a school organized in Germany (1919) to train craftsmen for industry.

Contemporary craftsmen, often schooled in the Fine Arts as painters, sculptors, designers, view the crafts in terms of creative challenge and place a premium first on form, then on utility. In many instances they pursue significant form, contending that this is their function. Their products reflect a great degree of inventiveness in the handling of a wide range of materials and processes usually associated with the crafts.

In recent years there has been an exciting renaissance in the area of crafts. Countless children, teen-agers, and adults everywhere are deeply involved in the self-satisfying act of making something with their hands. All phases of the crafts, including stitchery, weaving, mosaics, jewelry, ceramics, and textiles, have become a part of the current popular interest in producing hand-made objects.

Ideas, Design, Materials

An understanding of the role of the various crafts as a major influence in the history of man will add meaning to the student's personal efforts with crafts materials. From well-chosen examples of the work of craftsmen, past and present, the student also will become aware of design as an important part of this form of visual expression. How does the form of an object relate to its use? In what ways has the craftsman worked to integrate surface design with the object? What is the artist's basis for determining ideas to be interpreted in different crafts materials? How does the task of the potter differ from that of the weaver? The mosaic artist? The jewelry designer? When it is possible, members of local guilds and crafts clubs should be invited into the art room to show, discuss, and demonstrate their personal work and techniques. Trips to museums and stores, appropriate films and film strips will serve to enhance the total experience of the student as he considers his own ideas in the light of materials, tools, and processes.

In confronting the student with specific crafts problems, careful consideration should be given to:

Design

Working with the same visual elements that he would employ in any area of art expression, the student should strive for good visual organization, a sense of unity, and the quality of interest. Discuss the all-over appearance of the design, the relationship of the component parts to each other to produce harmony. How may the natural characteristics of the materials be utilized to enhance the design? How may the student's hands and the use of tools influence the design? Discuss the importance of surface treatment as a factor in the appearance of the object. The surface design of a three-dimensional object should be an integral part of the object; should enhance the total design. For example, oil may be rubbed into wood to bring out the beauty of the grain; a clear glaze, applied to clay to intensify the color and texture of a clay.

Function

The completed object should perform satisfactorily the task for which it was made. The student must analyze the problem, consider the materials to be used, and the structural elements necessary for satisfactory function of the final product. The demands in making ceramic jewelry vary from those related to cutting copper shapes for a bracelet. In either case the finished product must be made to stand the rigors of wear.

Ceramic Patio Light, courtesy Architectural Pottery, Los Angeles, California.

Ideas

Exposure to the work of craftsmen, past and present, will broaden the student's concept of crafts design and assist him in formulating his own ideas. Natural and man-made forms as well as subject matter may be used as a basis for prompting the student's imagination. Creative solutions to crafts problems are also influenced by function and the latent qualities of the materials used. Emphasize individualized response to a problem, personal interpretation.

Materials

Discuss the resident qualities of materials and how these qualities should be incorporated into the design to influence the final appearance of the product. Students should be given opportunity to handle materials to discover their potential and limitations. The interplay that is set up between the student, his idea, and the materials is an important factor in crafts design as in all forms of art expression.

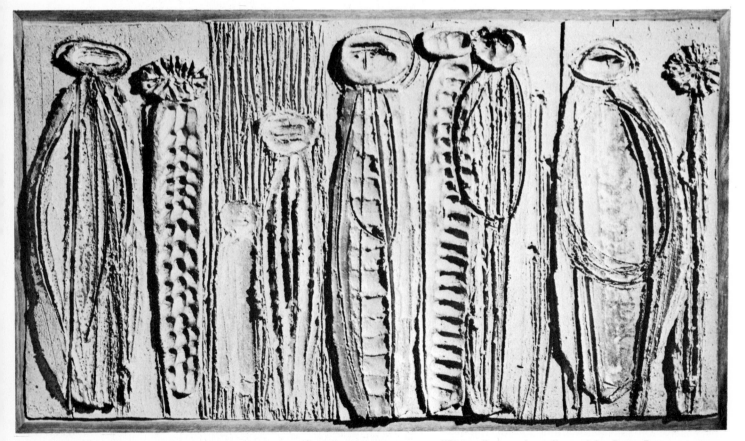

"Figures", ceramic wall panel by Betty Feves; courtesy American Craftsmen's Council, New York.

174

Craftsmanship

Good craftsmanship is essential to quality in design. Encourage a desire on the part of the student for thoroughness, careful construction, and finesse in his work. The completed product should reflect a certain skill in the use of the hands and of tools. An understanding of the process should be apparent in the design. Raggedness, resulting from lack of concern for good workmanship, only serves to detract from the design.

Pre-planning via the sketch will assist the student toward organizing his thoughts. Paints, chalks, and cut paper techniques are suitable for this purpose. Emphasize the importance of creating a general feeling for the design rather than attempting to simulate in the sketch the actual characteristics of clay, cloth, yarn, metal, glass, wood. Discuss design as it relates to form. How does the form of a three-dimensional object influence the surface decoration? A round bowl? A square object? In what way does a surface decoration on a container differ from a flat design in a mosaic? The design of a copper enameled brooch? In the preliminary sketch the student should determine what visual elements will be dominant in the design—linear qualities, shape relationships, color or value emphases, textural effects, subject matter versus non-objective interpretation of ideas. During the course of the pre-sketching stage, crafts materials should be available for simple explorations. An understanding of the nature of the materials will be influential in the determining of the design.

Since the materials used in making preliminary sketches will differ from those to be used in making the final product, the student will be involved in a new set of experiences as he translates his idea from sketch to product. During this process, he should be encouraged to work with flexibility, to make changes that may be suggested by the materials as he works with them.

In summary, crafts problems confront the student at once with creative design, function of product, personal interpretation, potential of materials, and good craftsmanship. The various crafts can be quite satisfying to the student at most grade levels. Simplified techniques and processes in early experiences should lead to more complex exploration later. At any stage of an expanding program of crafts, the marvelous feeling of personal expression is a reward to the student that can hardly be equalled.

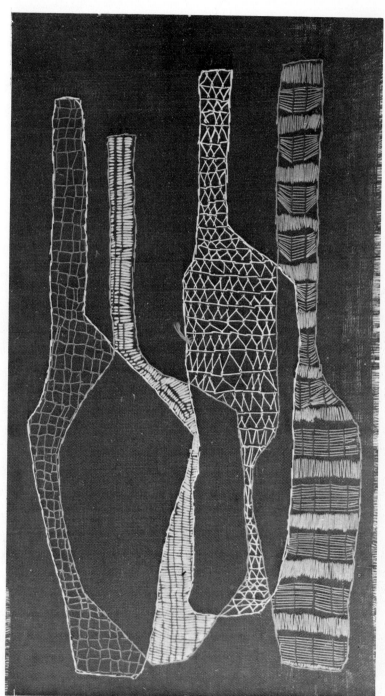

Stitchery, Baltimore City public schools, Maryland.

175

*Detail of a skirt, plain weave embroidered in stem stitch.
Peru, about 200 B.C.; courtesy The Textile Museum,
Washington, D.C.*

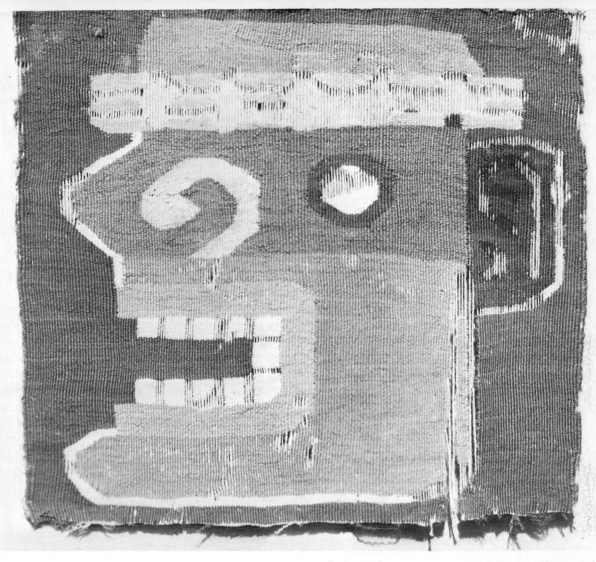

TEXTILES

Textiles, more often considered a minor art, have played a significant role in most cultures of the world. While the earliest efforts of man undoubtedly were directed toward the making of materials that would protect him from the elements, the concern for decoration was not to be ignored. Even in the joining of hides for personal wear, it is likely that primitive man experimented with various kinds of stitches, and not for their utilitarian value alone. Cloth fabrics from the venerable tombs of Egypt reveal a keen sense of design, typical of that era. The Third Century Coptic textiles are distinctive for their richness of quality; the work of the Peruvians, for their vigorous decoration. Intricately conceived animal and floral designs were characteristic of Byzantine artisans. The unexcelled masterpieces of the Oriental stand priceless today, particularly the expressively luxurious work of the Persians.

178   *"Mimosa", textile, designed by Henri Matisse; courtesy*
The Baltimore Museum of Art, Baltimore, Maryland.

Although it is not the purpose here to present the historical development of this fascinating craft, it is suggested that students become familiar with some of the highlights in the evolution of textile design. A number of books that treat the subject thoroughly are available. Museum trips, appropriate films, filmstrips, and reproductions may be used to increase further the student's concept of textile design, then and now. Point out the many different approaches to design in textiles; fabrics for utilitarian purposes as well as purely decorative or ornamental items; the role of textiles in religion, politics, and as a means for recording events.

Creative problems in textile designs may be divided into two major areas:

The creating of designs to be applied to the surface of a piece of fabric.

The creating of design to become an integral part of the structure of the fabric (weaving).

Students should be given the opportunity to work with the tools, materials, processes and techniques in both areas.

Designing on Fabric

Discuss with the student the purpose of the fabric design. Will it be used as a wall decoration? Converted into a handbag, a scarf, a tie, or belt? How would the design for drapery material compare to that for a skirt or blouse? Or place mats? Familiarize the student with various kinds of cloth that may be used from the coarse texture of burlap or monk's cloth to the finer weave of linen or unbleached muslin; canvas, netting, felt. Acquaint the student with the different techniques and processes that may be used to apply a design to cloth, including, stitchery, printing, batik, and free brush design. Emphasize the importance of good craftsmanship, simplicity of design, the integrity of the materials used.

STITCHERY

Drawing or designing with stitches offers unlimited possibilities for the student's imagination. Although there are hundreds of traditional stitches, only a few are necessary for most purposes. Encourage innovation rather than strict adherence to the conventional. Variety may be achieved by the texture and color of background material; by the weight and color of thread, yarn, embroidery floss, jute used in making the design; by stitching shapes of cloth to the background material (applique); by combining stitches with other processes, such as printing.

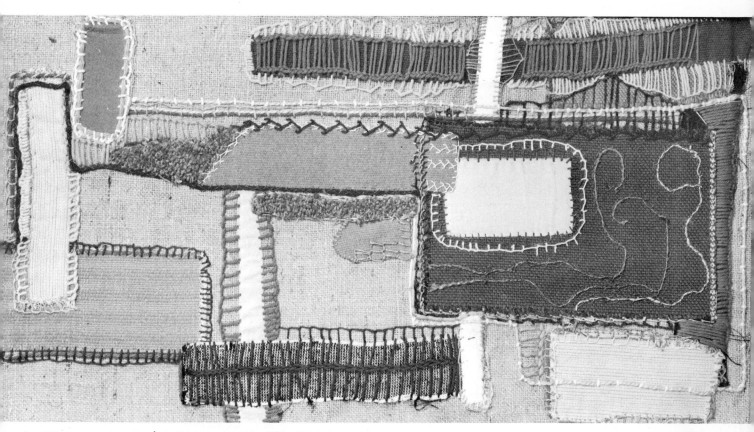

Stitchery and appliqué design; courtesy Lily Mills, North Carolina.

179

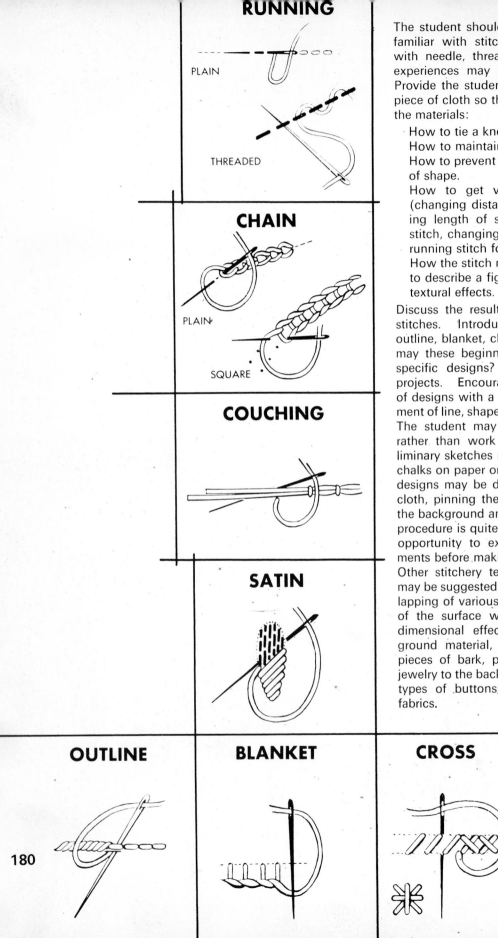

RUNNING

PLAIN

THREADED

CHAIN

PLAIN

SQUARE

COUCHING

SATIN

The student should have opportunity to become familiar with stitchery materials, to experiment with needle, thread or yarn, and cloth. Initial experiences may be limited to a single stitch. Provide the student with a length of yarn and a piece of cloth so that he may "get the feeling" of the materials:

How to tie a knot.

How to maintain proper tension on the thread.

How to prevent the cloth from being pulled out of shape.

How to get variation with a single stitch (changing distances between stitches, changing length of stitches, changing direction of stitch, changing kind of thread). Suggest the running stitch for this purpose.

How the stitch may be used to outline a shape, to describe a figure, to fill in an area, to create textural effects.

Discuss the results of this student search with stitches. Introduce additional stitches (cross, outline, blanket, chain, feather, couching). How may these beginning experiences be applied to specific designs? Consider individual student projects. Encourage spontaneous development of designs with a concern for organized arrangement of line, shape, color and texture.

The student may wish to pre-plan his design, rather than work directly with materials. Preliminary sketches may be developed with colored chalks on paper or with cut paper shapes. Some designs may be developed by cutting shapes of cloth, pinning them in a desired arrangement to the background and stitching them in place. This procedure is quite flexible and allows the student opportunity to explore many different arrangements before making a decision on the final step. Other stitchery techniques and procedures that may be suggested to the student include the overlapping of various colors of yarn; the building up of the surface with stitches, creating a three-dimensional effect; cutting through the background material, creating open spaces; caging pieces of bark, pebbles, broken glass, costume jewelry to the background; using various sizes and types of buttons; overlapping semi-transparent fabrics.

OUTLINE

BLANKET

CROSS

FEATHER

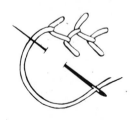

180

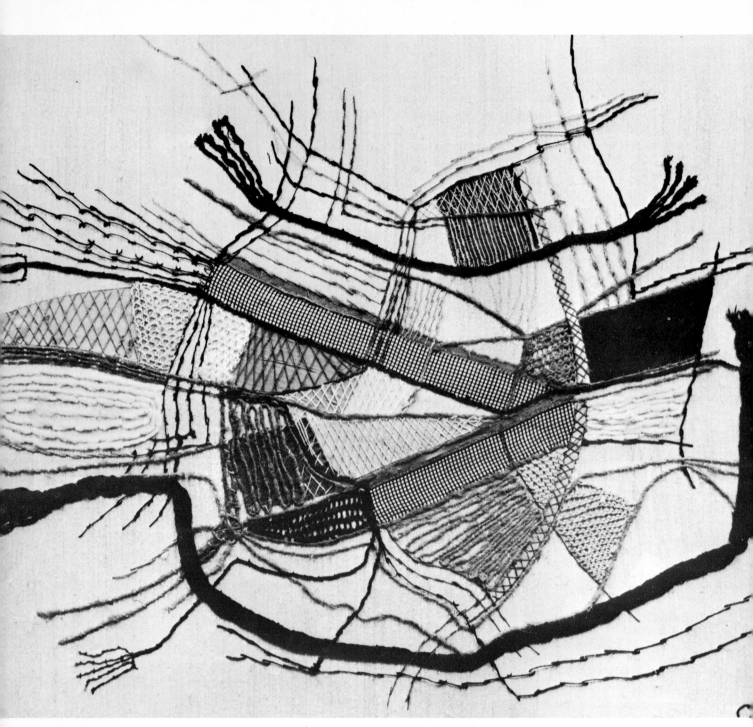

Embroidery by Mariska Karasz; courtesy American Craftsmen's Council, New York.

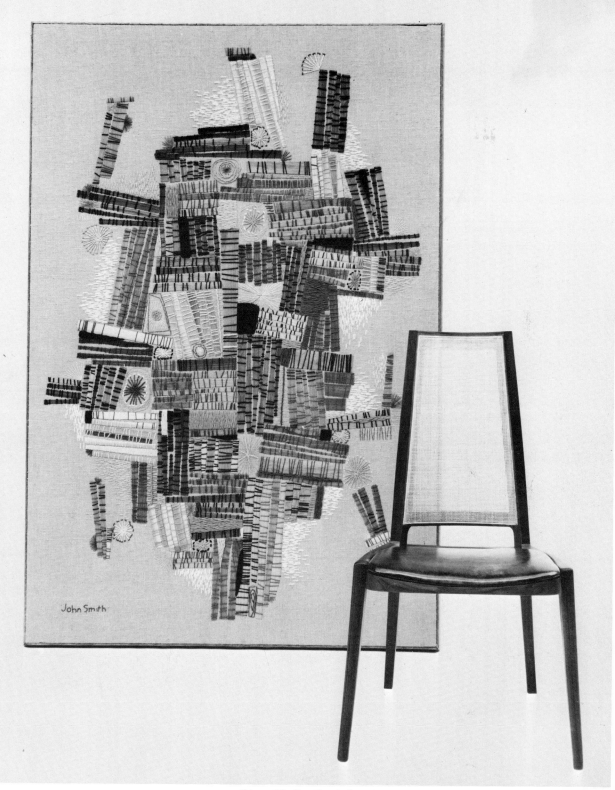

"Joseph's Coat", stitchery by **John Smith.** Dining chair handcrafted by John Kapel; courtesy Pasadena Art Museum, California.

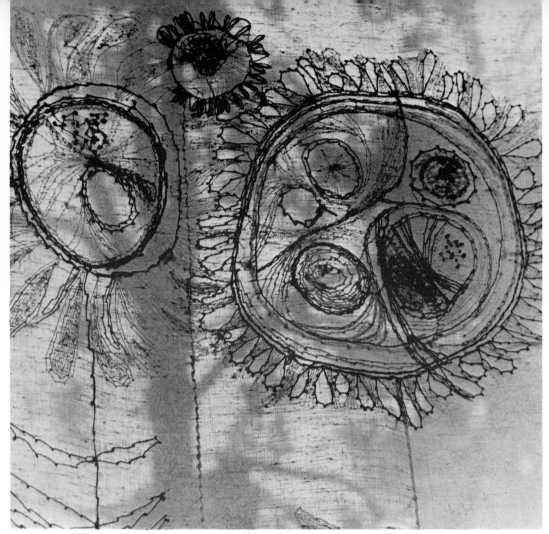

*Stitchery on casement, white, by **Eleanor Neil Coppola;** courtesy Pasadena Art Museum, California.*

"Cat Dreams", appliqué wall hanging by Carter Sassaman; courtesy American Craftsmen's Council, New York.

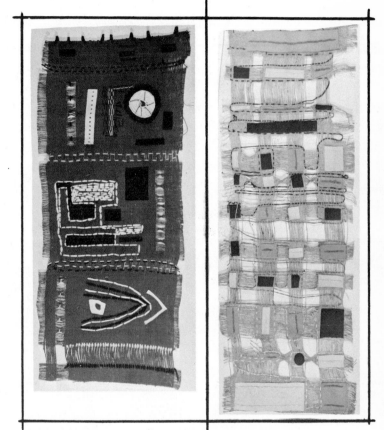

Wall hangings, combining stitches, applique, and open spaces produced by removing warp and weft threads of the burlap; Baltimore City public schools, Maryland.

St. George and the Dragon by R. Fumanski; courtesy Lily Mills, North Carolina.

185

The applying of a design to a piece of fabric with paints, inks, or dyes may be accomplished in many ways. A particular process such as batik may have its origin traced back many centuries. On the other hand, one of the methods more widely used by contemporary craftsmen, silk-screen printing, is of much more recent vintage. Whatever the technique, the use of paints, inks, or dyes on fabric provides the student with another approach to textile design that is somewhat different from his stitchery or weaving experiences.

Wall hanging, batik, by Joseph Almydo; courtesy American Craftsmen's Council, New York.

Printing

There are a number of printing methods that are suitable for transferring a design to a piece of cloth. Designs may be cut into linoleum, rubber, or wood blocks, inked and pressured onto the surface of the cloth. Stencils may be cut from a special ink-resistant paper and the color applied through openings or around shapes. Silk, stretched on a wooden frame, may be prepared by having parts blocked out to produce a design when ink is forced through it to the cloth surface. Designs may be developed, also, by using wood scraps, gadgets, or simple stamps made from erasers and vegetables (carrots, potatoes). Each of these techniques is described in detail in the chapter presenting printing techniques.

Discuss with the student the specific purpose of the design, the influence of the texture of the cloth (smooth to rough) on the design and on the printing process, bases for various repeat arrangements. Emphasize simplicity, basic shapes, interesting color relationships. All-over patterns are more suitable, ordinarily, for fabrics to be used as draperies, curtains, clothing, while representational themes may form the basis for wall decorations. In either case, stress the engaging flat quality that is characteristic of the printing processes used.

"Cats", fragment, plain weave. Peru, 1100–1400 A.D.; courtesy The Textile Museum, Washington, D.C.

Fabric designs by Herman Miller, Zeeland, Michigan.

Batik

In painting activities, the combination of materials such as crayon and India ink, crayon and water color, rubber cement and water color, to create a resist is quite popular. Because of the incompatibility of these mixtures, some rather unusual effects may be produced. Then too, the water colorist often uses rubber cement to block out objects in the foreground of his painting in order to lay a wash over the background.

The batik technique, used in textile design, is essentially the same process as discussed above. It is a resist method, of ancient origin, which combines wax with dye to create a design on fabric. The desired design is described on the cloth with wax. The cloth is painted with dye or immersed in a dye bath. The areas covered with wax are protected from the dye and remain the original color of the cloth. When several colors are to be used, the same procedure is followed for each color. Upon the completion of the design the wax is removed with heat or solvents.

Paraffin wax, melted in a container placed over a hot plate, may be applied to the cloth with various types and sizes of brushes or tjantings. The tjanting (available in many art stores) is a tool consisting of a bowl to hold hot wax and a spout to distribute the wax to the cloth. This tool may be used to produce fine lines. Small wood scraps, the ends of dowels, cardboard edges, sponges, and small objects may also be dipped into the melted wax and stamped on the cloth to create interesting effects. Common dye or waterproof colored ink are suitable for most batik purposes. The most satisfactory cloth for student problems is sheer cotton.

The student may work direct on the cloth or presketch a design and transfer it to the cloth with charcoal. It is recommended that the lighter colors be applied first. Succeeding colors will add to this as the design "builds." Discuss with the student the difference between immersing the cloth in a dye bath and applying the colors with a brush. Suggest that by painting there may be greater control in the selection and use of colors. Point out that whatever the procedure may be, the final result is achieved through a series of alternating applications of color and wax.

Tie-Dyeing

Another method for introducing a design on fabric is to push small areas of the cloth together, bind them tightly with thread, and dip the cloth in dye. The tied areas will not receive the dye. A variation is to fold the cloth and bind it before immersion.

Painting

Interesting and spontaneous designs may be developed on most fabrics by direct application of colors with brushes ranging from small camel's hair water color brushes to large house paint brushes. Variety may be achieved by allowing colors to run together, by dry-brushing, by spatter techniques, by working on damp cloth, by using inked rollers of different sizes.

Wall hanging, batik, by Berni Gorski; courtesy American Craftsmen's Council, New York.

Wall hanging, batik, by Ilono Bodo; courtesy American Craftsmen's Council, New York.

188

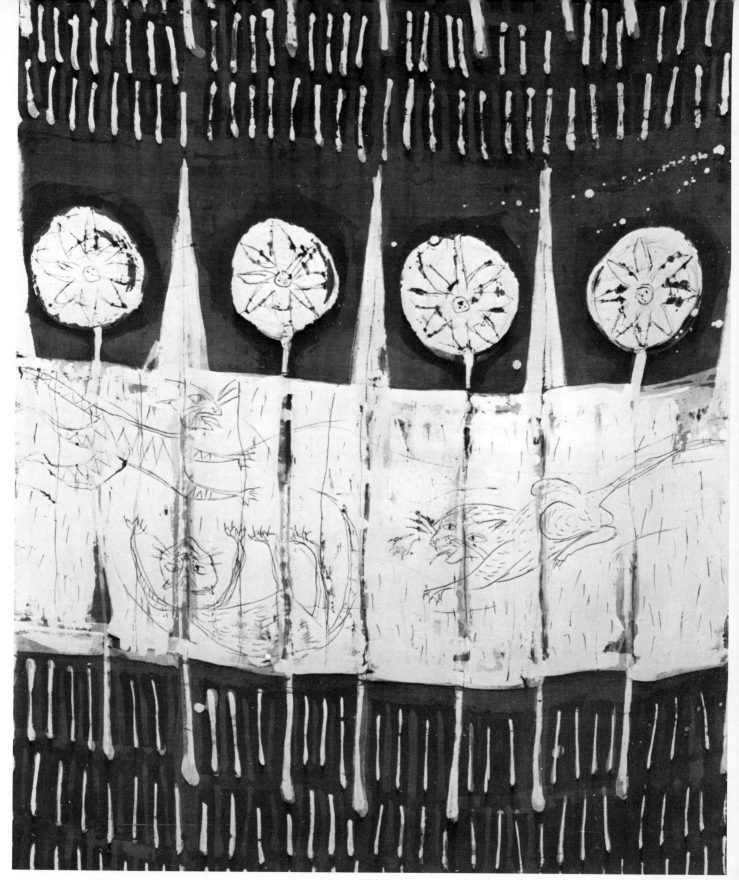

"Cotton Cats", batik, by Mary A. Dumas; courtesy American
Craftsmen's Council, New York.

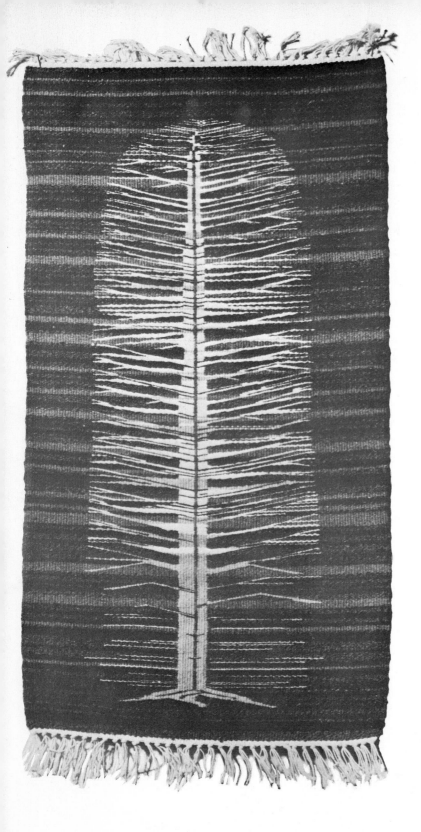

Tree Tapestry by Claribel McDaniel; courtesy American Craftsmen's Council, New York.

WEAVING

Textile design, created through the process of weaving, stems from a very early part of the stream of time as man knows it today. Yet the basic principle of interlacing a series of threads or fibers known as the *warp* with another series of threads or fibers referred to as the *weft* remains essentially the same.

Primitive man would stand aghast today before the endless flow of cloth from the highly mechanized looms of industry. What a contrast with the simple grass mats that he laboriously fabricated with his fingers alone! Thus the weaving process has evolved from the intertwining of grass and reed with no mechanical aids to yarns spun from animal and plant fibers to the adoption of the shed stick and heddle rod and to the invention of the hand loom to a supremely industrialized operation of the Twentieth Century.

Although the commercial weaving of textiles has reached a new high in mechanization to meet the demands of today's world, the craft as a means of individual expression has an allure for countless thousands of people around the world. Indeed, weaving is a fascinating art that brings a personal satisfaction that is at least equal to the other crafts.

Early experiences should acquaint the student with the fundamental concept of weaving, conventional techniques, basic weaves, appropriate materials, and specific terminology. Have the students examine examples of various kinds of cloth that may be obtained from local merchants. Discuss the apparent structure of the weave, the design as an integral part. Films, filmstrips, and museum trips when possible may be used to extend the student's understanding of the weaving craft, past and present.

Introduce simple hand weaving and braiding projects in which no loom is used. Provide the student opportunity to explore weaving with a rigid heddle loom that may be made with wooden tongue depressors; wooden frame looms and cardboard looms.

With this equipment the student will be able to weave ties, belts, scarfs, cloth that may be sewn into handbags and purses, place mats, and decorative textiles. Emphasize quality of design; organization of line, shape, and color; textural possibilities with various kinds of yarns, cords, cloth strips, raffia; experimentation.

SIMPLE LOOMS

Cardboard Looms—Heavy cardboard such as bookbinder's board cut to the size of piece to be woven; uneven number of notches cut in each end directly opposite to each other; warp thread strung across face of cardboard and around notches, ends tied together on reverse side. Experiment with variations of the regular over and under weave.

Wooden Frame Loom—A picture frame, a wooden box or four strips of wood nailed together with slits or nails on opposite ends to hold the warp threads.

Tongue Depressor Heddle Loom—A half dozen wooden tongue depressors, a single hole drilled through center of each; spaced approximately one-eighth inch apart and fixed at each end with two additional tongue depressors; eleven warp threads tied to stick and loose ends passed alternately through holes in and spaces between tongue depressors; loose ends then tied to another stick. With one stick anchored to a stationary object, the student fixes other end to belt or rope tied around waist, moves back until warp threads are taut, creates sheds by raising and lowering tongue depressor heddle.

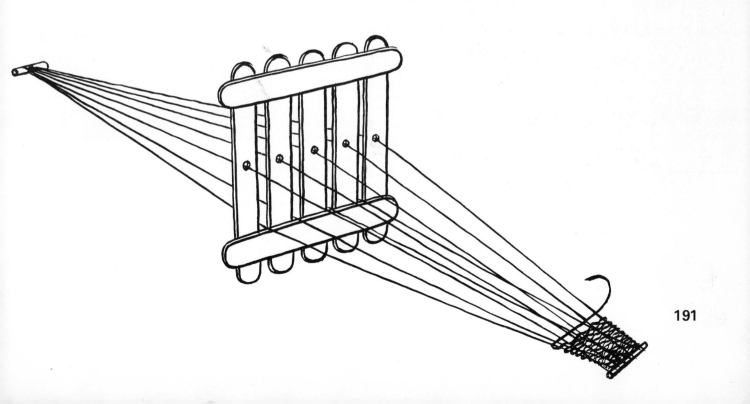

191

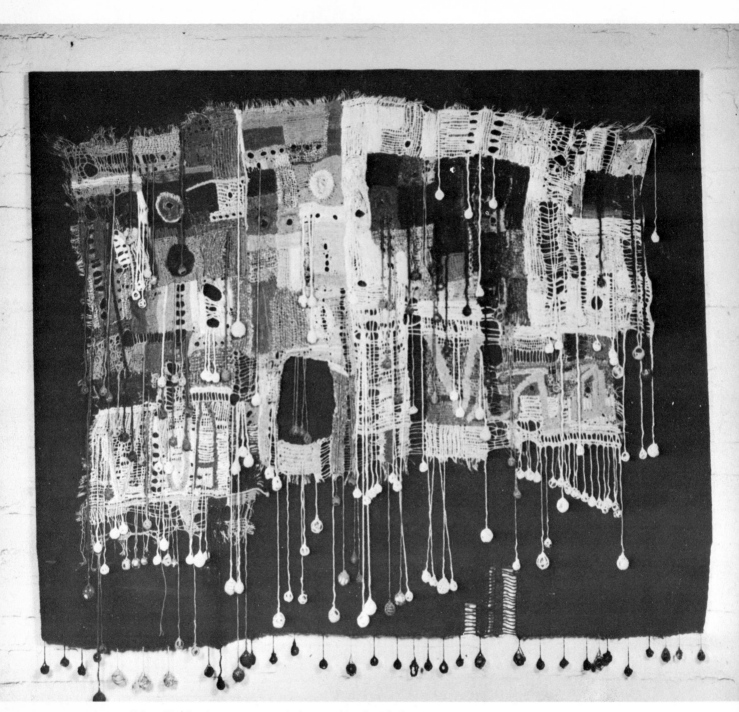

*"Viva, Viva," a banner, yarn and glass marbles by Marie
Kelly; courtesy American Craftsmen's Council, New York.*

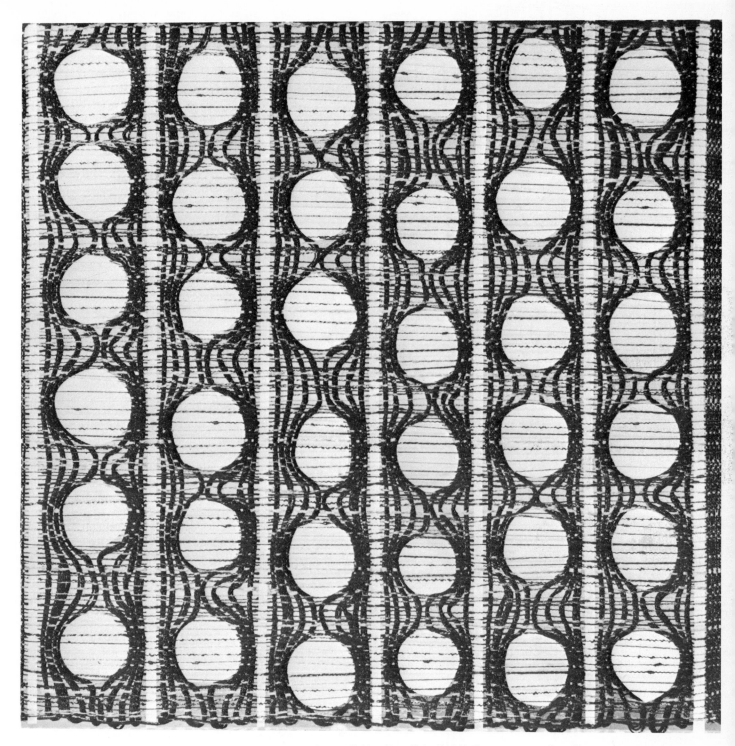

*Room divider (Detail) by Ted Hallman; courtesy American
Craftsmen's Council, New York.*

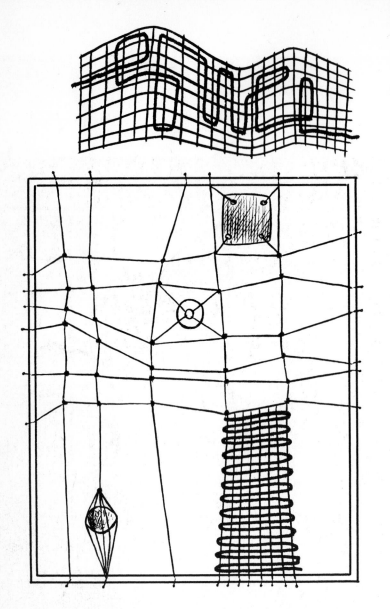

By looping, tieing, knotting, netting, and inter-lacing different weights and colors of string, cord, twine, jute, rope, the art room activity of weaving can assume an imaginative and creative posture. Some problems may be developed from basic weaving techniques; others, by merely handling materials in an inventive way.

For example:

Have the student string the warp thread on a wooden frame. Several colors of warp may be used. Create a pattern of shapes on this, leaving some background areas open. Empha-size color and textural relationships; turning the weft threads so that the warps are not pulled out of line.

Have the students experiment by tieing the warp threads to create an interesting pattern of lines. Develop solid areas with the weft threads or yarns.

Pieces of glass may be caged or woven into the design; also bits of costume jewelry, small metal objects, pieces of bark.

There are many possibilities for creative textile design over a solid backing such as a piece of masonite, framed with narrow strips of wood and coated with Gesso. Start with a few un-evenly spaced warp threads looped around nails in the top and bottom of frame. Create a pattern of space by pulling and knotting the warps with weft thread or yarn. At this stage of the design both warps and wefts should be kept taut to form a firm structure for the total design. Additional warps may be introduced in desired sections and woven in a conventional manner. Interesting objects such as washers, metal shapes, chunks of glass, may be woven or caged into different sections of the design. Solid areas of color may be painted in open areas.

A variation on this problem would be to develop simple shapes of color on the Gesso panel first, forming the textile design over this pattern. Colored tissue and PVA should be used for this purpose.

Provide the student the opportunity to weave on wire or cloth mesh. Fascinating three-dimensional effects may be achieved with wire mesh since it may be bent in different ways. The size of the mesh is a determining factor in the selection of weaving yarns, cords, or threads.

In summary, weaving experiences should fa-miliarize the student with weaving of the past and present; acquaint the student with conventional techniques of the weaver; and encourage an inventive attitude as the student becomes in-volved in this form of personal expression.

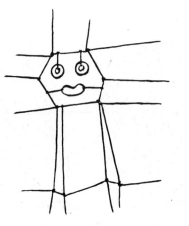

"Kukyrna" by Luba Krejci; courtesy American Craftsmen's Council, New York.

"Persona", stoneware sculpture by Betty Feves; courtesy Everson Museum of Art, Syracuse, New York.

CERAMICS

Man has used clay in the producing of ornamental as well as functional objects from the dawn of civilization. When or how he discovered this plastic material and put it to use is not known. However, some of the earliest primitive tribes left vivid record in pots, bowls, and jugs that have been unearthed in comparatively recent times. Indeed, it is through the ceramic crafts that the significant lines of artistic expression can be traced, even to the decorative pottery of the Stone Age.

It would be well to expose the students to some of the outstanding examples of ceramic ware of the past to increase their understanding of this art form as an essential product of the world's great societies. Reference should be given to the signal accomplishments of the Egyptians and the Aegeans; the asymmetrical design of Cretan pottery; the intimacy of expression in the painted Greek vases; the notable mastery reflected in Persian lustreware; the unexcelled contributions of the Chinese to ceramic art.

This "look" at examples of ceramic art should be extended to the work of outstanding contemporary ceramicists.

Greek vase, Sixth century B.C., Athenia. Kylix. Terra cotta; courtesy The Metropolitan Museum of Art, Fletcher Fund, 1927.

197

Ceramic Hippopotamus, Twelfth Dynasty, Egypt; courtesy The Metropolitan Museum of Art, New York.

Ceramic Owls; courtesy America House, New York.

DEVELOPING IDEAS

Clay offers the student a wide range of possibilities for translating personal ideas into three-dimensional forms. He may:

Produce a *clay pot* by pressing, pinching, and working a ball of clay in his hands until it is shaped the way he wants it; a *humorous figure* by adding clay to clay; a *capricious animal* by bending and cutting a clay slab into an unusual form; a *decorative tile* by pressing soft clay into a self-made plaster form; a simple tray by pouring liquid clay (slip) into an original plaster mold. Push, pull, roll, flatten, cut, join, add, take away, and carve in clay.

Use his hands alone, simple tools, or a power-driven wheel.

Add color; produce a matte or gloss finish; paint, stencil, stamp, or slip-trail glaze or underglaze colors to create a surface design.

Press interesting textures or patterns into the surface of his clay form with his fingers or modeling tools, nails, wire, spools, combs, sticks, and countless other objects.

Modify the surface of his clay object by adding thin coils, small shapes, strips, or balls of clay to form a design (appliqué).

Incise a leather-hard clay surface with a knife, clay tool, broken hack saw blade; excise leather-hard clay to create a low relief type of design that projects from the background.

Apply an engobe or a glaze to a clay surface and scratch a design into the surface (sgraffito). Use wax as a resist combined with thin coats of engobes or glazes to produce a surface design.

Provide the student opportunity to discover the innate characteristics of clay, to handle it, to see what he can do with it, to experiment with various simple forms (ball, roll, cube, egg-shape). Suggest that he cut one of these forms into segments, rearranging these smaller parts to produce a new, integrated form. He may hollow out or texture some of these segments to add variety. Have the student flatten this and roll the clay into a ball. Place two sticks ¼" thick on either side of the ball of clay. Using a rolling pin or large dowel, roll the ball out to form a slab. Develop various textural patterns on the slab with fingers, sticks, nails, nuts, bolts, combs, other small objects. What would happen to the clay slab if it were formed over a textured surface (wire mesh, corrugated board, burlap)?

Discuss the discovered characteristics of clay; its plasticity, its bulk, its solidity. In what way should these qualities of clay influence the student's design? Discuss the integrity of the material, how the design should reflect the natural properties of clay. Emphasize simplicity of design minus fine details; imagination, invention. Encourage the student to work with spontaneity.

198

Glazed ceramic sculpture; Florida State University School, Tallahassee, Florida.

*Four Figures, ceramic by Jan Van de Kerckhove, Belgium;
courtesy American Craftsmen's Council, New York.*

199

Ceramic bird; Lutheran High School, Los Angeles, California.

Ceramic design; courtesy Architectural Pottery, Los Angeles, California.

Family of bottles, stoneware by Philip Ward; courtesy American Craftsmen's Council, New York.

"Innocent City", *stoneware relief by Kenneth J. Dierck; courtesy Everson Museum of Art, Syracuse, New York.*

Preliminary exploration with clay coupled with an evaluation of the results will assist the student toward a more thorough understanding of the material. As the clay is being manipulated, the emerging form may suggest something to the student—a figure, an animal, a non-objective design. Fish, birds, masks, tiles, bowls, vases, ceramic jewelry, may also serve as bases for student ideas and projects in clay.

Clay activities should involve the student in the various conventional hand building procedures such as pinch method, slab, coil, coil-slab, wheel throwing, press molds, tiles. Adding surface decoration to greenware or to bisque-fired pieces should give the student experience in several techniques including carving or incising, stamping, building up, using engobes, applying glazes, painting, stenciling, slip-trailing, and sgraffito. However, while a knowledge of and skill in these areas is essential to the producing of a well-crafted object, a major emphasis should be placed on the student's personal expression in clay. This is necessary to avoid the familiar ash trays, "cute" figurines, and trite tiles that so often result from lack of sufficient motivation.

When is a pinch pot not a pinch pot? Provide opportunities for the student to probe this clay building technique as a vehicle for his imagination. How may a series of clay pinch pots be organized to produce an interesting, well-integrated form? What does a stack of three or four inverted pinch pots suggest? What may be added? Taken away?

A flat slab of clay, rolled out to an even thickness, can be an exciting challenge. From it a free form may be cut, draped over an interesting rock form (a can, a glass, or a plaster mound may be used), removed when leather-hard, and decorated. A similar free form may be placed in a hammock-like device formed by fastening a piece of cloth over the open end of an empty waste can or box. The shape that it will take depends on the tautness of the cloth. When the clay is leather-hard it may be removed and decorated. Material such as burlap or mesh will produce a textured quality on that part of the clay brought into contact with it. How may clay forms produced by the drape or hammock method be joined to enclose space? In what ways may this new form be modified to create a useful object? A purely decorative piece?

Suggest the use of a slab as a basis for figures, animals. Encourage humor and invention. Various parts may be formed to dry until leather-hard, then joined. Score and apply slip to both surfaces

to be joined. Emphasize simplification and minimum of parts to be joined. A great deal of interest can be achieved by bending, cutting, and twisting the clay.

Provide the student opportunity to draw on a slab of clay. Nails, sticks, and other pointed instruments are suitable for this purpose. Suggest drawing on a single tile or a series of tiles cut from the slab. A variation would be to express the idea by joining fine coils of clay to the surface of the tile. Stress the personal experience or imagination of the student as a basis for ideas.

Consider the cutting of shapes from the clay slab and building to create a non-objective form. How can interest be achieved by joining a number of similar shapes (5, 7, 9, etc.), whether the shapes should be the same size or vary in size, the introduction of a contrasting shape.

Have the students search out the possibilities of creating clay tile designs from plaster molds. The original design may be made with modeling clay or wax, over which the plaster is poured to form the mold. A number of tiles may be made from this mold by pressing soft clay into it. Progressive changes may be made by additional carving on the mold or by working on the clay design it produces.

Wheel throwing will provide the student still another kind of experience with clay. Considerable practice is necessary to become skillful in centering a clay ball on a wheel and raising it to form a wall of clay. A number of good books describing this technique are included among the references in this chapter. Although wheel throwing is a traditional method used in creating cylindrical forms, the student should be encouraged to seek out unusual designs by cutting, pressing, and re-shaping his wheel-thrown product.

In summary, this discussion has emphasized those procedures that will elicit fresh, lively, imaginative responses by the student to problems in clay. If his encounter with this extremely plastic material is limited to banal bowls, trite trays, and stereotyped statuettes, then he would best be spared the effort. Suffecent good references are supplied to describe such technicalities as preparation of clay, plaster bats, underglazing, glazing, stacking and firing a kiln, correcting imperfections.

Stoneware fountain by David Cressey; courtesy Pasadena Art Museum, California.

Ceramic fish; Lutheran High School, Los Angeles, California.

Ceramic bas-relief by Jan-Emile Derval; courtesy American Craftsmen's Council, New York.

Ceramic animal; courtesy Architectural Pottery, Los Angeles, California.

Cluster of pots, stoneware; courtesy Pasadena Art Museum, California.

"Not in Central Park" No. 3, stoneware sculpture by Jerry Rothman; courtesy Everson Museum of Art.   Permanent Collection, Syracuse, New York.

Ceramic design; courtesy Architectural Pottery, Los Angeles, California.

Antioch mosaic fragment depicting a head, Second century A.D.; courtesy The Baltimore Museum of Art, Maryland.

MOSAIC

The mosaic, a design form comprised of small tiles (tesserae) of stone, ceramic, or glass, was an important part of the esthetic life of the ancient Egyptians, Greeks, and Romans. Brilliantly colored tiles, pressed into wet cement overlayed walls and floors of public buildings, temples, and residences with designs of the times.

Although receiving substantial attention of artisans down through the years, the mosaic reached its perihelion in the sun of artistic achievement during the Fifth and Sixth Centuries. Fantastically rich surface decorations, covering the walls of Byzantine, Greek, and Italian churches, reflected the abounding influence of the artistic wealth of the East.

One of the earliest mosaic structures that remains in existence today is the Fifth Century tomb of Gallia Placidia at Ravenna. Still retaining much of their original extravagant splendor, these decorative prototypes show a concern for the pictorial as well as the ornamental.

Perhaps the most notable example of Byzantine architectural opulence, Santa Sophia, presents an interior, lined with a profusion of mosaic. Constructed in Istanbul during the Sixth Century, the structural elements of this monument to the ages were so formed as to provide the most effective application of mosaic.

DEVELOPING THE DESIGN

Surfaces to be covered with tiles have been extended beyond the walls and floors of ancient times to include various objects from ash trays to lamp bases, table tops to room dividers, three-dimensional figures and animals, wall decorations, and countless other items. Specific projects should grow out of the interests of the student. Age, experience, and depth of motivation of the student will serve as determining factors. Stress the same qualities of design and visual organization that prevail in other aspects of the art program. Particular emphasis should be placed on:

Flatness of pattern as opposed to subtle gradation of tone.
Broad, general treatment of surface rather than their intricate detail; potential and limitations of materials.
Shape, color, and value relationships.
Textural qualities that may be achieved by using tiles of varying thicknesses.
Effects achieved by space intervals between tiles. How does this differ from a design in which tiles are placed against each other?
Movement and interest created by the way tiles are positioned in the design.

Mosaic mural by Hans Hoffman. This mural encases an elevator core in an office building at 711 Third Avenue, New York City. Commissioned by the William Kaufman Organization; courtesy Lilly Associates, New York.

Appeal that results from irregularity in cut or broken tiles as opposed to the mechanical regularity of square commercial tiles.

The student may use colored construction paper or paint in making preliminary sketches for his mosaic. In these sketches, the student should seek out the general organization of his idea rather than attempt to cut or paint each individual tile. In transferring his completed sketch into actual mosaic material, the student should be encouraged to work with flexibility, making such changes as may be dictated by the materials themselves.

Themes or ideas for mosaic designs may range from recognizable subject matter to non-objective shapes. Discuss the relationship of the design to the specific purpose of the mosaic. A design for a tray would differ from that for a table top if for no other reason because of the contrast in size. Murals may depict school activities, sports, historical events or they may be designed merely to provide accents of color, shape, and texture in a school corridor. Stress the importance of the student's personal interpretation or style.

TOOLS AND MATERIALS

Commercially made ceramic and glass tiles (tesserae).

Other sources for tiles would be old ceramic dishes and colored bottles that may be broken into suitable sizes. Wrap the pieces to be broken in cloth and strike with a hammer or mallet. The cloth will prevent small pieces from flying and causing injury.

Small shapes of colored glass may be fired in a kiln to produce still another type of tile for class projects.

Commercial tilesetters ordinarily have surplus quantities of tiles that are of little use to them. A simple request may turn these tiles from a destiny on the city dump into an exquisite mosaic decoration.

Student-made ceramic tiles provide additional depth to mosaic projects. Roll clay, placed between two sticks 1¼" thick or more, to form a slab of even thickness. When the slab is leather-hard, apply the desired glaze. Using a knife, score the slab to form individual tiles. Place the prepared slab on a kiln shelf. Fire slowly in a vented kiln.

Pebbles of various colors, shapes, sizes.

Tile cutters.

Tile cement (glue such as Elmer's Glue and Duco Cement will serve the purpose).

Grout (to fill spaces between tiles).

Surfaces for flat designs (wood, plywood, pressed wood, plastic, bookbinders board).

The size, weight, and shape of the panel will be determined by the project. Unusual shapes of wood (from lumber yards or the Industrial Arts scrap box) often provide interesting bases for mosaic designs.

Section of mosaic mural by students of the Columbia River High School; Vancouver public schools, Washington.

210

PROCEDURES AND TECHNIQUES

There are two basic procedures that may be followed in fitting tiles into a mosaic design.

Direct Method

In this method the design should be outlined on the surface to which tiles are to be adhered. Spread adhesive over a small part of the surface to be tiled, cut tiles and press them into position. In some cases, individual tiles may be cut, and with glue placed on reverse side, pressed into position.

The use of grout is optional. However, it is advisable on designs that will have some specific use such as table tops. Grout will fix the tiles permanently in position in addition to giving the surface a more uniform appearance. Grout may be used natural (white) or have color (dry pigment) added. Grout mixed with water to the consistency of cream should be poured over the tiles and worked into the crevices. Remove excess grout with a cardboard squeegee. Allow grout to set, then wipe the entire surface with a damp sponge or cloth.

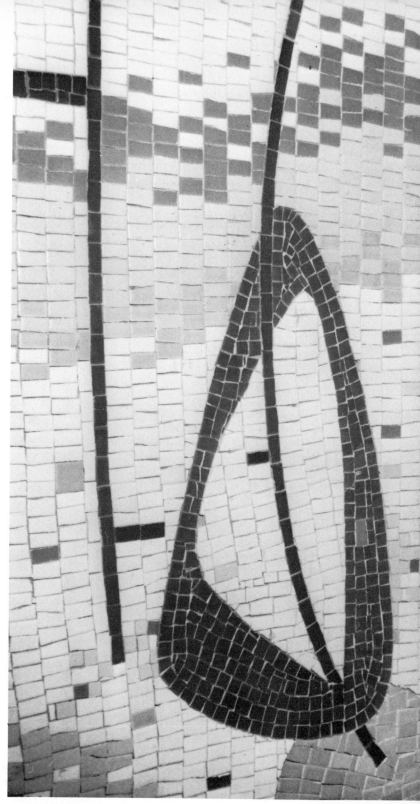

Mosaic table top (detail) made by the direct method.

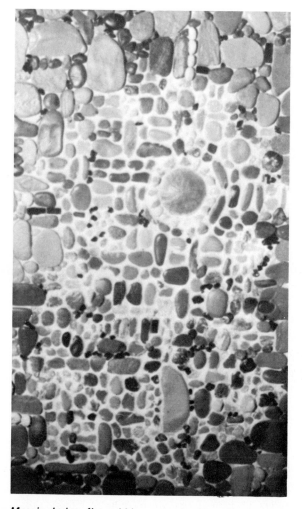

Mosaic design, flat pebbles, natural colors, direct method by Virginia G. Timmons.

211

Indirect Method

Outline the design, actual size, on a sheet of paper. Cut the tiles, placing them in position, face up, over this design. After all of the tiles have been cut and positioned, glue strips of water tape over the design, overlapping each strip. Coat the entire panel to which the tiles are to be adhered, with adhesive. Place the tiles on this surface with the tape side up. Press firmly into the adhesive and allow to dry. Remove the water tape and apply grout. A cement panel mosaic may be developed by placing the design, with tape side down, on a flat surface. Construct a wood frame to fit around the design. Pour cement (sand mix) into the frame. Wire mesh or metal rods may be pressed into the cement for reinforcement. When the cement dries, turn the block over, remove tape, and sponge with water. No grout will be necessary, the cement having worked its way down into the spaces between tiles.

Mosaic design, flat pebbles, natural colors, direct method by Virginia G. Timmons.

212

Wood mosaic; courtesy Pasadena Art Museum, California.

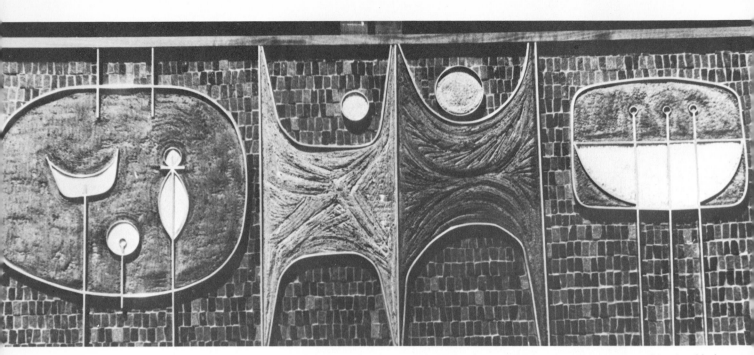

Mosaic panel. Brass, Venetian glass, marble, by Marj Hyde; courtesy American Craftsmen's Council, New York.

Altar Light. Stained glass, aluminum, brass, glass, walnut, by Philip D. Moore; courtesy American Craftsmen's Council, New York.

215

"The Web", mosaic panel by Irene Pasinski; courtesy
American Craftsmen's Council, New York.

Medallion: St. Peter, enamel on gold. Byzantine, Eleventh century A.D.; courtesy The Metropolitan Museum of Art, gift of J. Pierpont Morgan, 1917.

ENAMELING

The process of enameling, fusing of powdered colored glass to metal, was practiced in many ancient civilizations including the Egyptians, the Greeks, and the Romans. Yet it is interesting to note that it was not until the period spanning the Fifth through the Twelfth Centuries A.D. that the craft reached its high level of perfection. During this time, as with mosaics, it was the craftsmen of Byzantium who distinguished themselves by producing enamels that perhaps have never been surpassed. Vigorously patterned medallions, delicately colored reliquary casks, and richly ornamental bindings for the scriptures were among the many priceless treasures authored by Byzantine enamelists.

The enamels of this era were characterized by sharp divisions between the colors, brought about by gold cloisons which were formed by bending flattened gold wire to outline the design on the metal. Known as the cloisonné technique, the wire, secured to the metal background, enabled the craftsman to fill separate areas with different colors in paste form. The cloisons served as walls, preventing the colors from flowing together when being fired.

Later, the French and German enamelists, although influenced by the Byzantine craftsmen, developed another technique known as Champleve. Cells or recesses forming the design were cut into the metal surface, filled with enamel colors, and fired.

Other traditional enameling techniques of interest are Basse-taile, Plique-a-jour, and Limoges. The Basse-taile method is also one in which the design is cut into the metal and the recessed area filled with enamels.

Plique-a-jour is a technique in which a design formed with cloisons is filled with transparent enamels and fired. Having no metal backing, light will flow through giving a stained glass window effect. Similar results may be achieved by cutting openings in the metal and filling in with transparent enamels.

The Limoges method is simply the painting of the entire design on the surface of the metal and firing. The name is derived from Limoges, France, a town noted for its craftsmen and crafts schools during Medieval times.

Developing the Design

Student projects in copper enameling are limited only by the equipment and materials that are available. They may range from a simply decorated basic shape mounted on an alligator clip to serve as a tie pin to intricate three-dimensional forms using enameled shapes to produce a moving pattern of color. Trays, bowls, vases, wall decorations, constructions, paintings, and jewelry all offer fascinating possibilities for the student.

Although enamels may be fused on many kinds of metals such as steel, aluminum, and silver, copper is perhaps the most widely used metal. A lightweight copper such as 22 gauge may be cut with tin shears. Heavier 18 gauge copper would require the use of the jeweler's saw. For beginning projects small basic shapes and various sizes of trays and bowls may be purchased through local art materials suppliers. These may be used in introductory projects to acquaint the student with the process of enameling. (Avoid the stereotyped sea-horses, hearts, stars, etc.)

Pre-cut blanks are also good for jewelry such as earrings, cuff-links, pins, necklaces, and tie clasps. Copper shapes may be hammered to produce bowl forms by placing the copper shape over a shallow depression in the end of a wood log and striking it with a metal stake while turning it. A sandbag made of heavy cloth may be used as a substitute for the log. Additional refinement of the form may be achieved by turning it over a metal stake fastened in a vise and striking it with a planishing hammer.

The student also may explore the champleve technique by etching out his design on the copper shape, filling with enamel paste, and firing.

Another interesting technique that the student may consider is the paper stencil. This requires the cutting of the design from paper, placing it over a shape on which a base coat has been fired, dusting, removing the paper stencil, firing.

While these exploratory experiences will provide

"Tryptych No. 1", panel, printed enamel on copper by Arthur Ames; courtesy American Craftsmen's Council, New York.

217

the student with an understanding of the technical aspects of enameling on copper, the essential goal is to motivate him toward using this exciting art process as a vehicle for his own ideas. Provide the student opportunity to develop his ideas through preliminary sketches, cut paper and folded paper techniques. Emphasize simplicity of form, good visual organization, interest, and appropriateness of design for the enameling process. Consider the purpose of the piece to be crafted. Is it to be worn? To serve as a container? To become a decorative piece in a room? Show good examples of various ways that enameling techniques are used as an art form. Design problems should challenge the student toward the unusual. For example, small copper shapes or pre-cut blanks ordinarily become jewelry of some type. How may a series of enameled circles or squares be integrated into a pleasing design that may serve as a color accent in a room? Motivate the student toward seeking new meanings with an age-old craft.

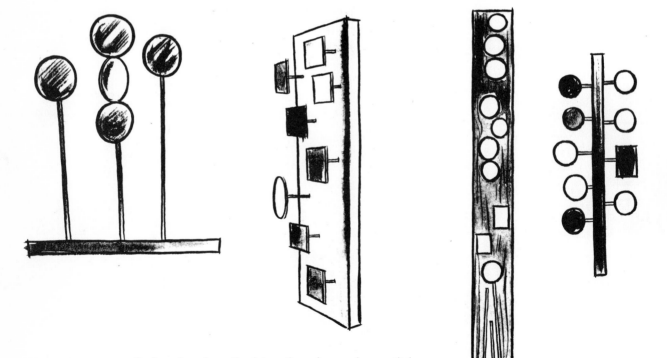

Designs based on the integration of several enameled shapes into a single unit.

Model of fountain for Children's Hospital, Pittsburgh, Pennsylvania. Enamel on brass, by Virgil Contini; courtesy American Craftsmen's Council, New York. A dominant feature of this design is the repeated triangular shapes.

CLEANING THE SURFACE, DUSTING POWDERED ENAMEL, INCORPORATING ENAMEL THREADS INTO THE DESIGN.

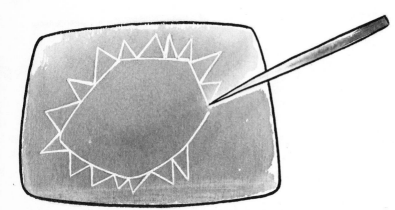

SGRAFFITO—SCRATCHING THE DESIGN THROUGH TO THE BASE COLOR.

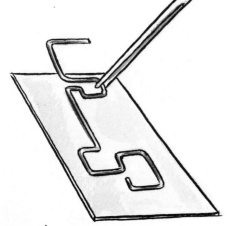

CLOISONNÉ—PLACING COPPER WIRE DESIGN ON A COPPER SHAPE PREPARATORY TO APPLYING ENAMELS.

Prior to engaging in specific enameling problems, opportunity should be provided the student to become familiar with the materials, some of the techniques used in applying enamels to copper, and the basic process itself. Through a guided search he will discover first hand the possibilities as well as the limitations of the craft. Pre-cut copper blanks or scraps may be used for this purpose. Such exploratory experiences should acquaint the student with:

Preparation of surface to be enameled—Steel wool, emery cloth, or a solution of 5% nitric acid and water may be used. Commercial solutions such as Formula 7001 greatly simplify the cleaning process. Without any preliminary cleaning, a thin coat of Formula 7001 prepares the surface for dusting and immediate firing.

Dusting—Powdered glass colors may be dusted on the copper surface by sifting them through an 80-mesh screen sieve. Coat the copper first with a thin layer of gum arabic or Formula 7001. The powder should be applied to the thickness of a thin dime.

Lumps and threads—Lumps or threads of colored glass may be arranged in interesting patterns to produce a design. They may be placed on top of a surface that has been dusted and fired or a base coat may be fired on the shape prior to the adding of threads and lumps.

Sgraffito—Fire a base coat of white enamel on the copper shape. After cooling, coat this surface with gum arabic or Formula 7001 and dust with a layer of powdered glass (dark color). Scratch a design into the base color and fire.

Painting—Fire a base coat of white enamel. After it has cooled, paint design with overglaze colors and fire.

Another painting technique is to paint design over a fired base coat with Formula 7001, dust with powdered glass color, remove excess, fire.

Cloisonné—Form the design with 18 gauge copper wire. Position it on cleaned copper shape and dust with flux. Fire. After this cools, fill the areas (cloisons) with an enamel paste (powdered glass and water) and fire again.

NOTE: In all firing the reverse side of the copper should be protected by painting it with a solution of one tablespoon of salt to one cup of water. (Commercially prepared protective solutions are available also.) This will prevent burning and scaling of the copper when firing.

Materials and Tools

Kiln—Enameling kilns range from simple hot plates with pyrex covers to front-loading furnaces with heating coils imbedded in their walls. A kiln for classroom purposes should be front-loading with a firing chamber measuring at least 4 x 8 x 8. It should have a pyrometer so that accurate temperatures may be determined.

Fork, firing rack, trivet, tongs, asbestos gloves; tweezers, hole punch, shears, jeweler's saw and blades (0 and 1), table vise, metal stake, planishing hammer, needle files, emery cloth, steel wool, shakes or sieves; copper sheets (22 to 18 gauge), copper shapes, solder, powdered enamels, lumps, threads, overglaze colors, Formula 7001, protective coating; also copper trays, bowls, 18 gauge copper wire (square), jewelry findings.

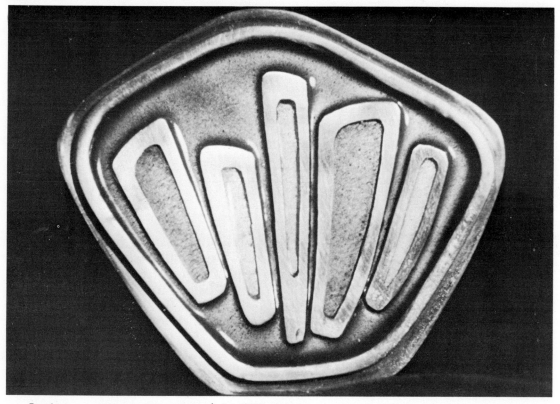

Pendant, enamel and silver cloisonné, by Sarita Rainey.

"Pomegranates" olive green enamel plate, sgraffito technique, by Kenneth F. Bates; courtesy Everson Museum of Art, Syracuse, New York.

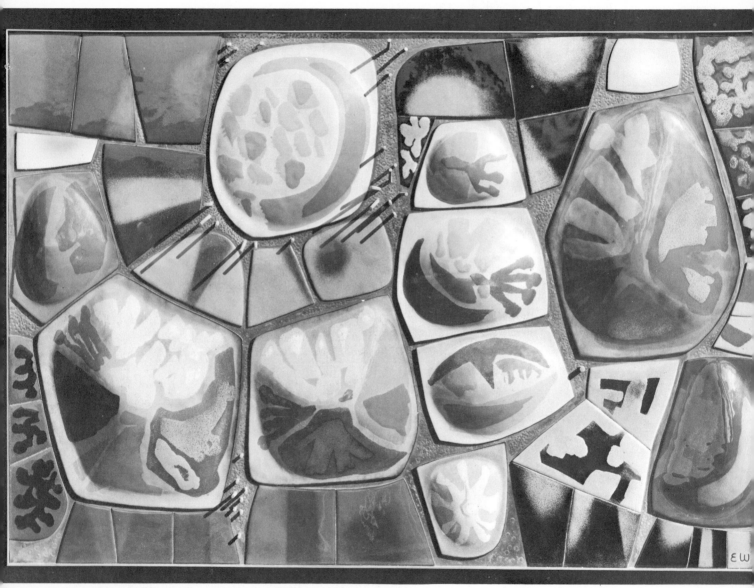

"Summer", enamel by Ellamarie Wooley; courtesy Pasadena Art Museum, California.

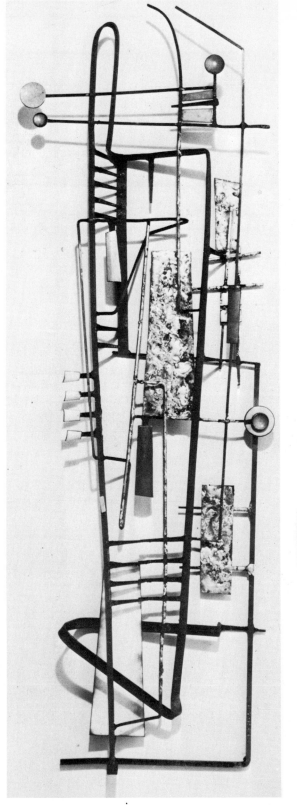

Construction, enamel on copper; courtesy American
Craftsmen's Council, New York.

"Floating Flounder", green enamel bowl by Mae M.
Conner; courtesy Everson Museum of Art, Syracuse, New
York.

Enamel painting: courtesy Pasadena Art Museum, California.

Detail from tryptych, "Resurrection" by Mary Ellen McDermott; courtesy American Craftsmen's Council, New York.

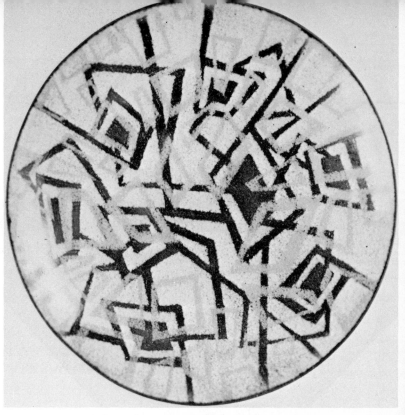

Enamel on copper by Sarita Rainey.

SUGGESTED REFERENCES: CRAFTS

Crafts Design

Moseley, Spencer; Johnson, Pauline; Koenig, Hazel; Wadsworth Publishing Co., Inc., Belmont, California, 1962. Well-illustrated, detailed description of designing with paper, bookbinding, weaving, textiles, leather, clay, mosaics, enameling, with an emphasis on quality in design and good craftsmanship; a good basic reference for a crafts program.

Creative Use of Stitches

Guild, Vera P.; Davis Publications, Inc., Worcester, Massachusetts, 1964. An excellent reference with a good variety of examples of creative needlework; includes materials, diagrams of basic stitches, things stitches will do, procedures for introducing stitchery projects, and techniques for motivation.

Adventures in Stitches

Karasz, Mariska; Funk & Wagnalls Co., 1959. Presentation of a variety of stitches including flat, looped, chained, knotted, detached, and composite stitches; excellent diagrams and illustrations, thorough treatment of stitchery stressing craftsmanship and innovation.

Create With Yarn

Beitler, Ethel Jane; International Textbook Co., Scranton, Pennsylvania, 1964. Presents the essentials of Hooking and Stitchery, including materials, equipment, and basic steps of each process; excellent illustrations; emphasis on creative design; inspirations for design and techniques for motivation.

Creative Textile Design

Harting, Rolf; Reinhold Publishing Corp., New York, 1964. An imaginative presentation of creative design with textiles; hundreds of examples of what can be created with simple textile materials.

Batik, Art and Craft

Krevitsky, Nik; Reinhold Publishing Corp., New York, 1964. A comprehensive introduction to fabric decoration; historical, traditional, and contemporary examples; detailed description of dyeing by immersion, direct painting of a batik, and using the tjanting.

Enameling for Beginners

Winter, Edward; Watson-Guptill Publications, New York, 1962. Thorough introduction to the art of enameling showing various steps through simple projects such as bowls, ash trays, plaques, and three-dimensional animals; excellent illustrations; includes detailed instructions on enameling techniques such as spraying, dipping, sifting, painting, slip and slush trailing, use of stencils, and sgraffito.

Weaving Without a Loom

Rainey, Sarita R.; Davis Publications, Inc., Worcester, Mass., 1966.

Ceramic Design

Kenny, John B.; Chilton Book Co., Philadelphia, 1962.

Creative Clay Design

Rottger, Ernst; Reinhold Publishing Corp., 1963.

Mosaic Art Today

Argiro, Larry; International Textbook Co., 1961.

Meaning in Crafts

Mattil, Edward; Prentice Hall, Englewood Cliffs, 1965.

Contemporary Interior; courtesy Knoll Associates, Inc., New York.

THE ESTHETIC WORLD: *Beyond the Studio*

The student moves in a world marked by the dimensions of height, width, depth. All three dimensions exist in the house or apartment in which he lives and in the architecture of his community. Even the small implements of his environment, such as tools and toys possess these qualities. The properties of color, texture, and line, as found in art, are also fused and related to this world. From the esthetic viewpoint, while a portion of this three-dimensional world is characterized by sensitive design, much of it possesses built-in ugliness. Yet this total man-made, machine-made environment, both good and bad, is a major influence on the development of the personal taste of the student. For it is from those things that are an integral part of his life, that he forms a basis for his judgments, his decisions, his present and future selection of one design over another.

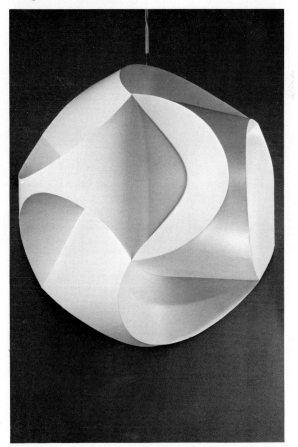

Light Sphere designed by Ben Gurule, California.

A modern apartment house in Milan, Italy; courtesy World Health Organization, Washington, D.C.

The man-made environment is indeed a significant part of the student and consideration should be given to design in the community as it relates to the various aspects of daily living. This would mean focusing the attention of the student on products of industry, new concepts in architecture, trends and directions in community planning, urban renewal, rehabilitation, conservation and preservation.

A look into the past will give evidence that a concern for these aspects of society has been a part of man for a long period of time. Exposure to and discussion of good examples from the past and present will assist the student toward an understanding of the motivating factors behind the making of tools and utensils, the building of an ancient temple, a Fifteenth Century cathedral, a Twentieth Century city. However, the emphasis should be on today! Highlight the new ideas, new images, new solutions, new materials, associated with the manufacture of tools, toys, furniture, home appliances, automobiles; the construction of commercial, industrial, public and private housing.

The Noxema Chemical Company building, Cockeysville, Maryland; courtesy Skidmore, Owings, and Merrill, Architects-Engineers, New York.

In some phases of this study of the world of man, the student's experience may be solely one of appreciation, analysis, and understanding. Yet, wherever possible, the student should be given opportunity to investigate materials in a search for his own personal solution to the design of things—a lighting unit, a toy, a handle for a tool, a kitchen in a low-rent, high-rise apartment. A study of local community planning efforts may lead to a group project resulting in drawings and a scale model of the target area.

Chairs; courtesy Herman Miller, Inc., Zeeland, Michigan.

Patio light; courtesy Architectural Pottery, Los Angeles, California.

Playground equipment; courtesy Jamison Manufacturing Co., Los Angeles, California.

233

MAN'S PRODUCTS

Products of industry, as we know them today, have a comparatively brief background; although tools, utensils, and objects designed for human comfort and convenience have a history that predates the earliest of written record. As a matter of fact, much that we know of ancient civilizations has been revealed through the work of their craftsmen. Throughout time, the artisan has been a prominent personality in various cultures and societies.

With the advent of the Industrial Revolution in the Nineteenth Century, hand-fashioned products gave way to the machine. Bigger and better and faster-producing giants of industry spelled the doom of the craftsman. Along with his exit, the concern for beauty of design was supplanted by a concentration on the machine and how much it could produce. Thus, the esthetic appearance of the product was completely sacrificed for its utility. It is important to note, however, that during this same period of time a concern was evident on the part of the Englishman, William Morris, and several others, for esthetics in industrial production. Morris attempted to produce in his workshop visually effective products for the masses.

Over the succeeding years, there developed a gradual recognition of the need for something more than usefulness and efficiency of the product. This, at first, led to timid and often awkward adaptations of traditional symbols to machinery and machine-made products in an effort to enhance them. These early attempts at product design, grotesque at best, provided the market with cast iron surfaces covered with floral designs, heavy industrial machinery with stanchions modeled after ancient Greek columns, classical sculptural forms as structural elements in a clock case.

Gas range, 1916.

Cast iron gas range, 1899.

Simplified design of the 60's.

Today, much attention is assigned to the design of the product, the creating of the corporate image. Beyond the manufacturing process, the engineer and the industrial designer often function as a team. They explore ideas, develop new concepts of appearance that ultimately determine the shape of the product, whatever it may be. Regardless of how successful a design may be today, the industrial designer thinks in terms of tomorrow, plans revisions, seeks exciting changes. The industrial designer must know the likes and dislikes of the public, the techniques of production, technological advances that affect his design. To perform his task effectively, the industrial designer must understand the function of the product, the characteristics of materials to be used in manufacturing the product, and the manufacturing process.

Familiarize the student with some of the utilitarian products of the past (tools, weapons, utensils). Discuss the relationship of product to need, to the nature of materials. How have technological advances and scientific discoveries affected the shaping of products? Relate these understandings to the machine-made products of today. Discuss some of the movements and personalities that have influenced today's industrial design, such as the Bauhaus (1919), Germany; Henry Dreyfus, Norman Bel Geddes, Mies van der Rohe, Eero Saarinen, Raymond Loewy. Trace the changing design of a product over the past several years (home appliances, automobiles, trains, airplanes, furniture). How have new materials, including synthetics, played a part in the evolution of a design?

Provide the student opportunity to study and redesign man-produced products. Tools, toys, utensils and some appliances may be brought into the art room for examination and analysis. The student may pre-sketch his design ideas, then transform them into three-dimensional materials. Many of the materials suggested for sculptural problems would be suitable for these experiences (wire, wood, paper, metals, plastics, clay).

DESIGN in the evolution of the telephone. From left to right, the common battery phone of 1900; the desk set, 1910; the touch-tone telephone of 1964; courtesy the Chesapeake and Potomac Telephone Co. of Maryland.

Design a container to hold a breakable object (light bulb or glassware). The final test would be to drop the package to see if it met this objective. Design a source of light for an entrance hall, for a table, for a desk. A major objective would be to provide sufficient amount of light to meet specific needs.

Design a storage space for books. Consider the possibilities of a self-standing, hanging, or wall-mounted structure.

Design a handle for a tool, a utensil, a door. The shaping of handles for tools may be developed through the shaping of a piece of plasticine so that it feels comfortable to the hand. This may be cast in plaster and further refined or shaped in wood.

Re-design an appliance. An appliance is similar to a package in that the outer shell must be shaped to house something. A toaster may be described generally as a container for heating elements combined with space for slices of bread.

Design a structure that will provide comfortable seating.

Have the students bring from home an inexpensive item which indicates the influence of the industrial designer. Such items as small tools, pens, ash trays, a spoon or even objects on their person such as, a purse, a watch, a pencil may be evaluated and serve as a basis for a design problem.

In all design experiences, emphasize the function of the product, suitability of materials, relationship of the design to the manufacturing process; simplicity of design and good craftsmanship. Define specific problems so that they will encourage invention and imagination.

Chairs; courtesy Herman Miller, Inc., Zeeland, Michigan.

Horse-drawn fire engine, late 19th C.; courtesy the Seamen's Bank for Savings in the City of New York, Antique Bank and Toy Collection.

MAN'S PRODUCTS REFLECT THE AGE IN WHICH THEY ARE BORN

Playground equipment; courtesy Jamison Manufacturing Co., Los Angeles, California.

Merry Oldsmobile, 1902–04.

Oldsmobile, 1919.

Chevrolet, 1940.

Photographs on this page courtesy General Motors Corporation, Detroit, Michigan.

Firebird IV.

"Roto" chair; courtesy Dux, Inc., Burlingame, California.

Light designed by Elsie Crawford, Palo Alto, California.

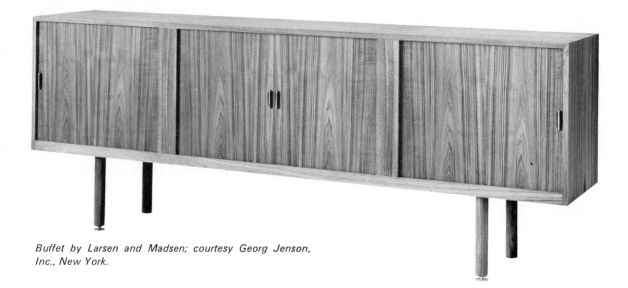

Buffet by Larsen and Madsen; courtesy Georg Jenson, Inc., New York.

Table; courtesy Herman Miller, Inc., Zeeland, Michigan.

Playground equipment; courtesy Jamison Manufacturing Co., Los Angeles, California.

Concrete benches designed by Elsie Crawford, Palo Alto, California.

MAN'S DWELLING PLACE

A look into the past would confirm the fact that man has directed unending effort toward shaping better, more convenient, and more efficient places in which to live, work, play, worship, and to administer his way of life. In the relatively simple life of pre-historic man, a hole in the side of a hill, a natural lean-to, or a tree served as a basis for his daily operation. What a contrast with the comparatively complex but extremely functional apartment unit common to today's urban community! The intervening centuries reveal countless changes, innovations, and refinements that are an essential part of the evolving architecture of diverse cultures, societies, civilizations.

Standing in testimony to this unrelenting drive of man to build a better, a more desirable physical

Beach house by Jock McKay, architect, California.

environment is a stream of monuments that reflect his ingenuity and inventiveness as well as his failures, shortcomings, and oversights. Pyramids, temples, public buildings, cathedrals, castles, palaces, towers, bridges, skyscrapers; vast metropolitan complexes of industry, business, finance; luxury apartments, public housing, suburbia—all are a part of our architectural past, present and future.

A study of architecture should acquaint the student with outstanding examples of the past and how they fit into a pattern that reflects an evolution of architectural forms rooted in the scientific discoveries and technological advances of man. Consideration should be given to basic forms of construction which would include the dome, masonry as compared to structural steel, the principle of the cantilever, prefabrication; the importance of these developments in relation to architectural style in different eras. Discuss the influence of society, government, and the church on architecture in various cultures and civilizations of the past. What effect has climate, available materials, and economic conditions had on the product of the architect? How have painting, sculpture, and other art forms been correlated with architecture of the past? This exposure to the historical role of architecture should provide the student with a greater insight into interesting societies of history, and a broader basis for understanding the importance of architecture today.

At Kowloon, next to Hong Kong, where most of the new buildings are going up, building sites have to be hacked out of the mountainside. Photo courtesy World Health Organization, Washington, D.C.

A particular emphasis should be placed on concepts of architectural design today; personalities such as Eero Saarinen, Frank Lloyd Wright, Edward Durell Stone, and countless others who have given leadership in the architectural revolution of the Twentieth Century; new materials and the fresh use of traditional ones; the integrity, plasticity and function of today's architecture designed to serve more efficiently human activity and living. Compare present day structures with those of the past; the more direct enclosure of space in contrast with, generally, the more involved and massive practices employed in constructing buildings of the past; the simple expressiveness of a modern multi-colored office building against the brash ornateness of other eras. Consider the many types of structures demanded by business, industry, religion, recreation, government, and private life and the many variations. For example, private residential construction ranges from low to moderate to high income families; row houses, walk-up apartments, high-rise apartments, ranch houses, split-levels, and many other classifications designed to meet the needs and requirements of today's society. Discuss those factors that guide the architect in his search for new ideas: human needs—physical, social, economic and esthetic; physical environment, land; influence of natural forces and commercial services (gas, electricity, sewerage); available materials—wood, stone, metals, glass, laminated and pre-cast materials, plastics; coordination of interior with exterior, of total design with surrounding environment; mass, shape, color, and texture as important visual elements in the unified organization of space. Discuss the procedures of the architect from preliminary sketches to floor plans, elevations, and final concept.

Home office, Phoenix Mutual Life Insurance Co., Hartford, Connecticut. Architects, Harrision and Abramovitz; builder, George A. Fuller Co.

Beinecke Rare Book and Manuscript Library, Yale University, New Haven, Connecticut; courtesy Skidmore, Owings, and Merrill, Architects-Engineers, New York.

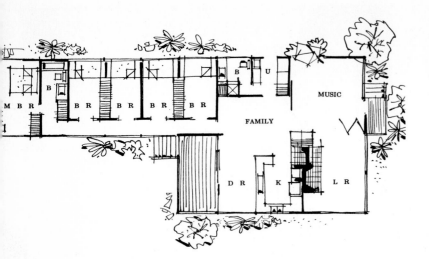

Floor plan of Dave Brubeck house.

It is possible, sometimes, to invite a local architect or builder into the art room to discuss the various aspects of his work. Other sources of basic information, trends, and illustrative material may be found in national magazines and trade journals that are oriented specifically toward architectural design. Plan sketching trips into those areas of the community where there is new construction. Provide opportunity for the student to investigate enclosure and division of space as it would relate to a specific architectural problem (a one-bedroom apartment, a studio apartment, the re-design of the interior of an old house, the art room, the design for the entrance to a local commercial, industrial, or church building). Problems such as these should involve the student in analyzing the requirements, making preliminary sketches, floor plans, and possibly a scale model.

Dave Brubeck house; courtesy of the architect, Thorne.

Bold in concept, the structure, through the cantilever, seems to soar, giving it a "tree-house" effect.

246

Northwestern National Life Insurance Co. building,
Minneapolis, Minnesota. Architect, Minoru Yamasaki.

Emhart Corporation building, Bloomfield, Connecticut;
courtesy Skidmore, Owings, and Merrill, Architects-
Engineers, New York.

Chase Manhattan Bank Plaza Rock Garden; courtesy Skidmore, Owings, and Merrill, Architects-Engineers, New York.

THE ARCHITECT SEEKS UNITY BETWEEN
THE INTERIOR AND THE EXTERIOR

Corridor, Chase Manhattan Bank; courtesy Skidmore, Owings, and Merrill, Architects-Engineers, New York.

Today's architect is confronted with demands that go far beyond the design of a single structure. Urbanization in the United States and around the world is progressing at a rapid pace. Expanding metropolitan areas with their promises and accompanying frustrations are seen on all continents, in countries that have been developed as well as those that are under-developed, in new nations and old.

What are the factors that are significant to the growing metropolitan complexes? To megalopolis? Several basic forces that have contributed to the rapid growth of cities are the lure of industry, high birth rate—low death rate, increasing possibilities from expanding government agencies, better educational facilities and opportunities and many additional amenities of the big city. Discuss the characteristic problems that have resulted from the population explosion within urban areas. (1) The natural gravitation of newcomers toward the central part of the city has resulted in overcrowding, slums, inadequate and sub-standard living facilities. "An estimate made by the United States Municipal News and based on United States conditions indicates that every 1000 new people in a metropolitan area require: 4.8 elementary school rooms, 3.6 high school rooms, 8.8 acres of land for schools, parks, and play areas, an additional 100,000 gallons of water per day, 1.8 new policemen. 1.5 new firemen, 1 additional hospital bed, 1000 new library books, a fraction of a jail cell, sewerage and treatment for 170 pounds of organic water pollutants per day" (Based on a report of the World Health Organization, December, 1964). (2) The extensive pollution of the atmosphere and of water caused by industry, increased needs of the population, and the swift growth of motor transportation threatens individual health and has harmful effects on land areas and agricultural crops. (3) Inter-urban traffic as well as transportation within the city presents problems of congestion and safety that are seemingly insurmountable. (4) Increasing background noise in cities is a contributing factor in mounting nervous and mental disorders. This has had significant influence on planners and builders seeking new solutions to construction and establishing satisfactory standards of control.

On the premise that the health of man depends on the health of nature (and vice-versa) metropolitan planners are concentrating on techniques and controls that promise something better than a veiled sun, fetid air, lukewarm and filthy rivers and harbors, and earth deprived of its green mantle. Magnificent buildings, totally new concepts of architectural design, open space, green areas, traffic control and transportation innovations, improved health conditions, all are becoming more and more evident in the changing face of man's dwelling place.

Urbanization in the United States and around the world is progressing at a rapid pace.

Housing project in Italy; courtesy World Health Organization, Washington, D.C.

On the spot experiences in the community will help the student toward a greater understanding of the need for metropolitan planning and of his responsibilities now and in the future, in relation to urban renewal projects. Ordinarily local agencies and committees make available pertinent films, filmstrips, charts of target areas and other visual materials. Acquaint the student with the various phases of community or city planning: (1) Urban Renewal (demolition of existing structures and re-building). (2) Rehabilitation (refurbishing of existing facilities within a neighborhood). (3) Different types of public housing. (4) Industrial parks. (5) Provision for business interests. (6) Traffic patterns. (7) Municipal, educational, and recreational requirements. What is the role of the architect? Discuss the different concepts of design reflected in local urban renewal projects, those in other areas of the United States and around the world.

Suggested projects:

Sketching and painting trips in the inner city.

Before and after sketching trips in areas undergoing rehabilitation.

A concentrated study of a single target area within the community. This would indicate a group approach with class committees gathering information such as population requirements, public utilities, traffic patterns, churches, schools, municipal buildings, shopping areas, provisions for recreation; conferences with the city planning director; survey of the area to be studied.

Plans for a low-rent apartment; an emphasis on designing living spaces within a limited part of a building.

Design for inner-city fountain and park or green areas.

Design for a playground in an urban residential area.

Redesign of an existing row house.

Most of these projects should involve the student in preliminary sketches, color sketches, scaled elevations and floor plans, scale models.

The "before" and "after" of an urban renewal project; courtesy the Baltimore Urban Renewal and Housing Authority, Baltimore, Maryland.

Low income public housing is an important part of the city's renewal program.   Photo courtesy Baltimore Urban Renewal and Housing Authority, Baltimore, Maryland.

AN IMAGINATIVE ADVENTURE IN URBAN REDEVELOPMENT

Photos courtesy Greater Baltimore Committee, Baltimore, Maryland.

Air view of model of Baltimore City's Harbor Development Project.

Two additional views of model of proposed plans for redevelopment of the harbor area, Baltimore City.

Architect's rendering of park area to be developed in
Charles Center, Baltimore, Maryland.

256

*One Charles Center; first building to be completed in
Baltimore City's Charles Center Project.*

Model of World Trade Center to be built in Lower Manhattan, New York.

Proposed marina and boatel on East River near Battery, New York City.

Plans for new Pace College campus, Beekman Downtown Hospital, and apartments, New York City.

SUGGESTED REFERENCES: THE ESTHETIC WORLD

Pioneers of Modern Design
Pevsner, Nickolaus, The Museum of Modern Art, New York, 1949.

Space, Time and Architecture
Giedion, Sigfried, Harvard University Press, Cambridge, Massachusetts, 1956.

Face of the Metropolis
Myerson, Martin, Random House, New York, 1963.

Architecture: City Sense
Crosby, Theodore, Reinhold Publishing Corp., 1965.

Contemporary Architecture: Its Roots and Trends
Hilberseimer, L., Paul Theobald & Co., 1964.

The Death and Life of Great American Cities
Jacobs, Jane, Random House, Inc., 1961.

Art and Industry: The Principles of Industrial Design
Read, Herbert, Indiana University Press, Bloomington, 1961.

ORGANIZING ART PROGRAMS
Quest for Quality

In the previous chapters of this book, an effort has been made to present the broad aspects of the major areas of art expression which form the content for student experiences in the visual arts. While this analysis of art forms is by no means an exhaustive one, a particular emphasis has been placed on a qualitative encounter with two- and three-dimensional design rather than one that is essentially quantitative. The references that form the bibliography have been carefully selected on the basis of their thorough treatment of specific topics and their support of high standards of design quality and craftsmanship. There are no gimmicks, no prescriptions, no recipes for the teacher who is seeking a short cut to easy success.

Providing a basis for each chapter are those fundamentals that are significant to any meaningful experience with art form. Consideration is given to the traditions of art, the visual elements, the qualities that give validity to design, the distinctive terminology that is essential to visual literacy, the materials, tools, techniques, and processes that are vital to the work of the artist, and suggested art experiences designed to develop student attitudes of adventure and discovery and feelings of genuine personal accomplishment.

No attempt has been made to write a program for a typical community, school, or group of students. Indeed, it would be impossible to outline a detailed program of art at any one grade level that would meet the needs of art teachers from one school system to another. However, there are some very basic considerations that will be discussed here in the hope that they may serve as guidelines in the organizing of art programs at various grade levels in any school environment.

The Values of Art in the Program of Education

Art education has played a variety of roles in the public school curriculum. Its values, objectives, goals, and its methods for accomplishing its purposes have changed from time to time to meet the changing demands of the evolving American community.

The earliest art programs emphasized the importance of drawing as training for the mind and hand. Later, influenced by the requirements of industry, mechanical drawing became a part of some school programs. At another point in the growth of art education, art was advocated as a force in molding character, in building refinement. The progressive education movement of the

Art education broadens the boundaries of the student's experiences.

Twentieth Century advanced the premise that art education provided for emotional release, facilitated identification with self, and fostered creativity.

Art education, from its inception has taken numerous roles, has shifted its values frequently, and has changed its concepts of its means and its ends according to the needs of the times. This is one of the most valuable lessons that may be derived from the history of art education. Yet there are many indications that the art programs of today are very much a part of a past philosophy. Elliot Eisner,* Associate Professor of Education and Art at Stanford University, made this observation. "I believe that the curriculum in art education in American schools, insofar as one is able to generalize about it, is a hand-me-down from another era and from another decade. I believe that our programs are programs that reflect the values and objectives of the progressive educators and the progressive movement generally. The curriculum of art education and the purposes of art educators are wedded to the development of creativity." From the beginning of the progressive education movement in the 1920's and 1930's, art education assumed the role of chief advocate and promoter of creativity. In the decades that have followed, art programs, art guides, art educators and art conferences have placed major emphasis on art education as a means for promoting creative attitudes in the students. The literature of art education has been profound in its endorsement of creativity as a paramount virtue, a central goal of the program of art education. Art teachers have referred to creativity as an element that is peculiarly the property of the art curriculum. Creativity has become synonymous with art education.

While there is no quarrel with the merits of creativity, it would seem that there is a need to consider it in relationship to recent trends in general education. Art education has no exclusive patent on creativity. The whole realm of education, with its edge of traditional methodology somewhat blunted in recent years, has assumed an attitude that reflects a greater concern for the creative abilities of the student. Science, Mathematics, English, Languages, and numerous other subjects are making great strides in stimulating the student's capacity to think creatively.

An analysis of current art education practices which are directed toward cultivating creativity

Students learn about the materials, the tools, the techniques, and the processes used by the artist.

in the student may reveal that efforts to produce an esthetically sensitive individual have not been completely successful. It should be noted that paralleling the growth and establishment of the creative concept (and many times exceeding it in importance) has been the tremendous increase in the number of art activities accompanied by an overwhelming variety of materials. Many art programs today can be measured almost entirely by the amount of gluing, soldering, tieing, bending, cutting, sawing, pouring, dribbling, spattering, pressing, mixing, and tearing that a student may accomplish with balsa wood, toothpicks, wire, string, pipe cleaners, newsprint, scrap materials, plaster, paint, clay, wheat paste, and colored tissue. While there may be some therapeutic value in this quantitative "art" environment, it leaves much to be desired in terms of the depth and quality of the student's personal relationship to art forms, his creative responses, and his maturing level of esthetic sensitivity. It would appear that art education in many respects has become the victim of creativity, through the program it has generated, rather than an effective force for meaningful creative expression.

At this moment in the Twentieth Century, the United States is enjoying the greatest economic prosperity, the highest scientific achievement, and the most incredible technological advances ever known to man. Education stands on the threshold of new challenges, exciting frontiers,

261

*Elliot Eisner, "Curriculum Ideas in a Time of Crisis," *Art Education*, October, 1965, Volume 18, No. 7, p. 8.

and unexplored horizons. Scores of programs sponsored by the Federal Government have given new impetus to the entire scope of education, to research, to pilot studies, to specialized courses, to cultural advancement. This would suggest a re-examination of the visual arts in an attempt to determine the values that art has to offer in the forming of the well integrated, visually literate personality. It is on these values that the long-range objectives of the art program must be structured.

In substance, a contemporary philosophy of art education should mirror the needs of the community, the school, and the student. Manuel Barkan states that "We may assume that the values to be derived from the arts depend on how experience through the arts best serves the purposes and needs of today's children."*

Art activities should provide the student with a qualitative experience with art materials.

What are some of the values of art education that are significant to the preparation of the student for his place in a society characterized by its vigorous change?

Art education, with its humanistic qualities, tempers the popular emphasis on material well-being. The student's awareness of the value of esthetic experience, developed through contact with the ideas, symbols, and forms of the artist as well as through personal performance can make him wiser than he otherwise might be.

Art education contributes to the intellectual and cultural maturity of the student. Through his developing knowledge of the art of the past and present, the student gains a greater insight into past cultures and a more sensitive understanding of the function of art in today's world.

Art education develops in the student an ability to criticize discerningly, thereby improving his own position in society and in turn that of society itself. Art experiences (appreciative and productive) increase the student's level of sensitivity to design, generate more sophisticated attitudes toward art form.

Art education provides a new dimension to the student's personality and broadens the boundaries of his experience. Art activities nurture the student's creative and imaginative capacities, develop in the student a spirit of inquiry and adventure in his search for a personal response to a problem. The uniqueness of art education is that it provides for the need to be unique.

Art education increases the perceptive and the manipulative competencies of the student. Through meaningful experiences in art the student becomes visually aware and increasingly capable of meeting standards of quality in his own work.

In summary, these values stress the importance of the student's attitudes, understandings, sensitivities, responses, and skills as they relate to the visual arts and to his place in life. This suggests an art program that gives appropriate attention "to skillfully-guided, esthetically-oriented creative expression and to the development of the pupil's understanding of works of art produced by professional artists."*

A Qualitative Program of Art Education

The consensus of opinion among many art educators and much of the current literature on art education is that there should be a greater emphasis on quality of content and experience

*Manuel Barkan, *A Foundation for Art Education*, The Ronald Press Co., New York, 1955.

*Howard Conant, New York University, Seminar on Elementary and Secondary School Education in the Visual Arts, 1965.

in the art program, less concern with activities that have limited educational benefit for the student. This does not imply that the performance aspects of the art program should be minimized, but that they should be brought into a closer relationship with the cultural, historical, and critical elements of art expression.

In general, art programs should be organized to provide for: (1) A comprehensive involvement of the student with the art products of man (Painting, Sculpture, Architecture, Graphics, Crafts), (2) An intelligent basis for making value judgments, and (3) A qualitative relationship of the student with tools, materials, and processes utilized in his personal visual expression. These are distinctly interrelated conditions that are essential to the development of the student's attitudes, understandings, sensitivities, and productive abilities in art.

The Art Products of Man

In bringing the student into contact with the traditions of art, stress the humanizing qualities of the art products rather than the accumulation of facts arranged in chronological order. In this way, the experience becomes a means for building the personal values of the student through intelligent association with the best in art expression.

Emphasize the relationship of the artist and his ideas and forms to his time, to his particular culture; the influence of tools, materials, and technological discoveries on the artist and on the shape his product takes; the significance of painting, sculpture, architecture, crafts and other art forms in the stream of history.

The student's expanding knowledge of the art products of man will assist him toward more qualitative responses in his own experiences with materials when this study is integrated with the productive aspects of the art program. For example, a selection of paintings representing different movements in the history of art and diverse styles of interpretation will assist the student toward a greater realization of the personal relationship of the artist to his work. From this experience the student also will become aware of basic concepts of visual organization and of the extensive range of techniques employed by artists.

Bases for Making Value Judgments

The student's concept of design will reach a higher level of sophistication as he becomes more sensitive to the visual elements and the qualities of good design. This cannot be achieved through memorization of pre-determined definitions nor through the completion of stereotyped exercises (charts, color wheels, diagrams). It must be cultivated within the context of the art product. Through critical analysis of art forms the student will gain new insights into the meaning of visual order and will acquire the necessary skills to make value judgments. The student's ability to interpret, to criticize, to make choices with discrimination, is based on his internalized feeling for line, shape, space, color, value, texture, unity, contrast, movement.

A particular emphasis should be placed on correct art terminology; a concerted effort, on its specific application. These are the tools with which the student communicates his ideas, and on which he bases his esthetic choices.

A Qualitative Relationship With Tools and Materials

Creative expression does not occur in a vacuum. The student's ability to create successful art products is dependent upon his attitudes toward art, his knowledge of art form, his understanding of esthetic standards, and his perceptive and manipulative competencies. The art program should be outlined so that it will assist the student toward the acquiring of basic art information, skills, and techniques that will lead to a more satisfying personal expression.

The art program should have the kind of continuity that will provide a meaningful relationship between what was done, what is being done, and

263

Adequate time should be provided for the student to develop skills to be used in his own visual expression.

what is to follow. The students should be involved in art activities that build on their previous experiences, skills, and techniques. At the same time, the students should know where they are going, how their present activity fits into the total program of art.

The art program should have a sequence of performance activities that require an increasingly complex response by the student as he progresses. Repeated activities with identical goals, skills, materials, and tools are deadening to the student.

The art program should provide adequate time for the student to develop skills related to various aspects of art expression. In this way the student will gain greater control of the materials, tools, and processes used in his personal visual expression.

The art product that the student produces is important to him. In a sense, it is a reflection of his spirit of adventure and discovery; the sum of his maturing sensitivity to visual order; an indication of his personal standards of quality of craftsmanship. It is the student's reaction to his total art experience. The success or failure that he meets in his own performance is influential in the forming of his attitudes toward the visual arts.

These components of a quality program of art obviously would not be assigned the same degree of emphasis at each stage of the educational process. The very young child is content with symbolizing his environment. As he progresses toward maturity he requires more than an opportunity to express himself. Therefore, in the defining of specific goals and in selection of content for the program, consideration must be given to the levels of knowledge, sensitivity, experience and comprehension of the students.

The Art Teacher

The key to quality in the art program is the teacher. Values, goals, and objectives may be defined and modified at times to reflect changing emphases in the art program. Specific courses may be instituted, guides written, suitable arrangements made for tools, supplies, equipment, and art room facilities. An elaborate organization of instructional materials, including the latest developments in such media as single concept devices, programmed techniques, and educational television may be available to the school. Yet in the final analysis, the effectiveness of the art program may be measured by the performance of the art teacher.

The key to quality in the art program is the well-organized, enthusiastic—often unpredictable—art teacher.

What are the characteristics of a good teacher? What ingredients are essential to excellence in teaching?

One characteristic of the good teacher is his personal, genuine enthusiasm for art as a significant force in the ultimate maturity of the student. The good teacher projects an enthusiasm that is catching; an enthusiasm that "rubs off" on the student; an enthusiasm that excites and inspires the student. The effective art teacher conveys to the student that art is important, even indispensable. He generates a feeling that the unique act of creating with materials is exciting, vital, momentous, urgent.

Then, too, the good art teacher has confidence in his ability to perform effectively, the self-assurance that he is equal to the task. He manifests a presence that is implicitly positive. He believes in his subject, its values, its purposes, its worthwhileness.

Essential to quality teaching is that the teacher must have a comprehensive understanding of the basic content of the art program. This would imply that his knowledge of the traditions of art, his understanding of visual organization, his concepts of design, and his competency with tools and materials must be extensive. The broader the teacher's experience in the whole range of art expression, the more effective he will be in his own ability to teach.

The importance of thorough planning and organizing of a meaningful, sequential program of art cannot be over-emphasized. Quality teaching just does not happen when the art teacher operates from an "off the cuff," spur-of-the-moment, "instant" lesson plan. Each aspect of the art program must be related, thoughtfully, to the level of knowledge, experience, and skills of a specific group of students. Consideration should be given to the areas of art expression to be taught, the objectives to be achieved, the materials to be used by the students, the mechanics for handling art materials and student work, techniques to be employed in implementing specific lessons, definition of art problems, time for student response, and the relating of the work of the students to established goals. The thoroughness of pre-planning is reflected in the attitude of the students toward art and the quality of their art products.

While the lesson plan forms the basis for the development of the lesson, the approach used by the teacher to put the plan into effect should be a major source of inspiration for the students. The imaginative, inventive teacher tries the un-usual in communicating his ideas to the students. He utilizes teaching procedures that infuse the art room environment with a spirit of adventure and discovery. Students become bored with "sameness." The good art teacher is often unpredictable, cannot be anticipated, does the unexpected. Students look forward to being in his presence. This level of teaching involves more than an effective use of films, filmstrips, bulletin boards, visual materials, demonstrations, and other media currently being adapted to the educational process. Good teaching is generated by the total personality of the teacher, his manner of expression, his movement throughout the art room, his desire to search and to explore ideas, his sincere interest in and enthusiasm for art, and his concern for the students.

Finally, quality teaching is a product of a positive professional attitude. The good art teacher has a deep-rooted concern for the values of art in the growth and development of the child and for his own personal role in this process. He is open-minded, seeks new ideas, and keeps informed. He is sensitive to the total educational program, the students, the other teachers, the administration, the parents, the community. The good art teacher is actively interested in professional organizations, advanced study, research, continuous self-improvement. He views teaching as a vital force in the community, a lively, creative profession. The good art teacher is dedicated to the task of teaching and simultaneously is engaged actively in the pursuit of excellence in his own teaching techniques.

SUGGESTED REFERENCES:

Bulletin Boards
Horn, George F.; Reinhold Publishing Corp., 1962.

How to Prepare Visual Materials for School Use
Horn, George F.; Davis Publications, 1963.

Teaching Secondary Art
Lanier, Vincent; International Textbook Co., Scranton, 1964.

Creativity and Art Education
Brittain, W. Lambert; The National Art Education Association, Washington, D.C., 1964.

Creative and Mental Growth (Revised Ed.)
Lowenfeld, Viktor and Brittain, W. Lambert; the MacMillan Co., New York, 1964.

Art: Search and Self-Discovery
Schinneller, James; International Textbook Co., 1961.

A Foundation for Art Education
Barkan, Manuel; The Ronald Press Co., New York, 1955.

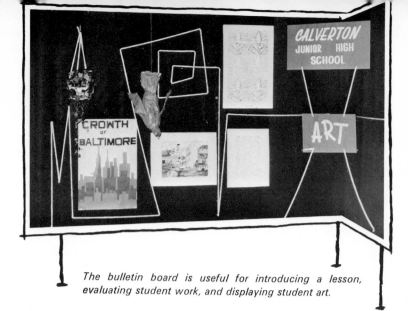

The bulletin board is useful for introducing a lesson, evaluating student work, and displaying student art.

Demonstration of techniques, skills, and processes assists the student to a more thorough understanding of the art form.

Visual, made by mounting cards, containing major points of a lesson, on a packing box. The box may be turned during the presentation, showing each step in sequence.

Display panel used in the presentation and later as a basis for the critique.

The uniqueness of art education is that it provides for the need to be unique.

267

*Stoneware bottle by George Roby; Everson Museum
Permanent Collection.*

INDEX

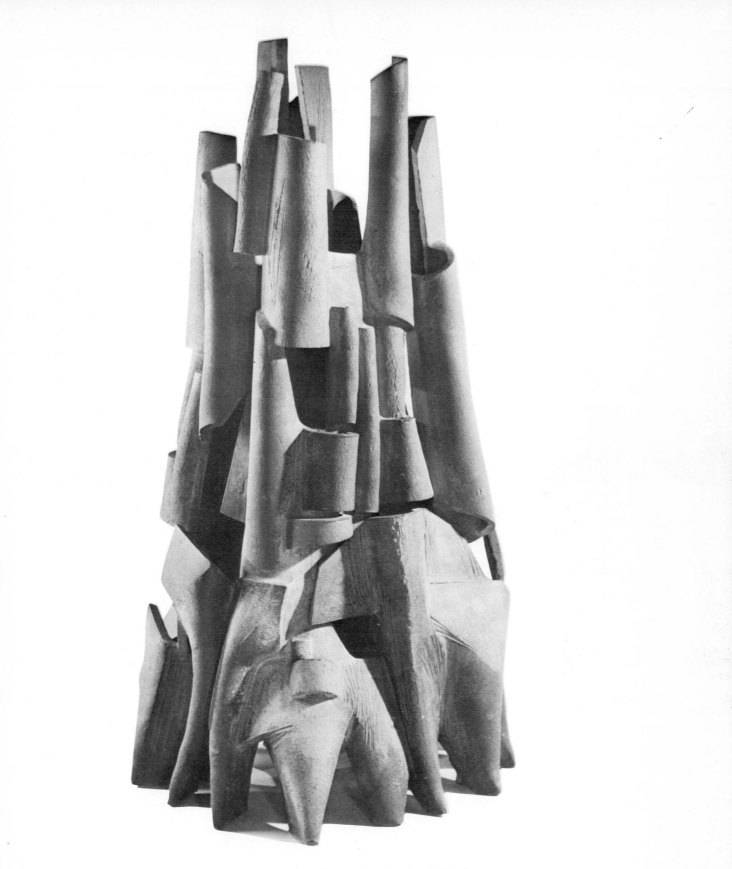

"Megalith"; courtesy Architectural Pottery, Los Angeles, California.

I am most grateful to Mrs. Virginia G. Timmons, Mr. James A. Schinneller, and Dr. Ivan E. Johnson for carefully reviewing this manuscript. Their comments, recommendations, and suggestions have been most helpful in the final organization of the text.

Many illustrations contained in this book showing art of the past as well as that of more recent artists have been obtained through the kind cooperation of several museums. I wish to express my appreciation to the following: The Philadelphia Museum of Art, Hobart L. Williams, Executive Assistant to the Director; The Textile Museum, Washington, D.C.; Frobenius-Institut, Frankfurt, Germany, Dr. Walter Resch; The Phillips Collection, Washington, D.C.; American Craftsmen's Council, New York; The Pasadena Art Museum, California, Eudorah M. Moore, Curator of Design; The Baltimore Museum of Art, Maryland, David McIntyre, Assistant Director; Alinari, Florence, Italy; Instituto de Antropologia, Veracruz, Dr. Alfonso Medellin Zenil; The Museum of Modern Art, New York, Richard L. Tooke; Addison Gallery of American Art, Phillips Academy, Andover, Massachusetts, Bartlett H. Hayes, Jr., Director; Everson Museum of Art, Syracuse, New York; Metropolitan Museum of Art, New York City.

For their generous cooperation, I wish to thank the following artists, craftsmen, business, and government agencies who supplied me with an abundance of excellent illustrative material for this book: America House, Ltd., New York; Peter Askin of The Durst Organization, New York; Baltimore Urban Renewal and Housing Agency; Columbia Broadcasting System, Inc., New York; Elsie Crawford, Palo Alto, California; J. H. Cromwell, The C. & P. Telephone Co. of Maryland; Downtown-Lower Manhattan Association, Inc; Dux Incorporated, California; El Merriam, Inc., Los Angeles, California; Fire Drum Corporation, San Francisco, California; John L. Friskey, Baltimore Gas and Electric Co.; Merle Froschl of *Seventeen* Magazine; Greater Baltimore Committee; Gurule, Los Angeles, California; Italian Tourist Information Office, New York; Warren Jamison, Jamison Manufacturing Co.; Delbert Jones, Lippincott and Margulies, Inc.; John A. Kapel, Designer, Woodside, California; Knoll Associates, Washington, D.C.; Damon Lawrence of Architectural Pottery, Los Angeles, California; Lilly Associates, New York; Lily Mills, High Point, North Carolina; Brooks Marshall of General Motors Corporation; Jock McKay, Architect; McManus, John, and Adams, New York; Herman Miller Furniture Co., Zeeland, Michigan; Herman Miller Textiles, Michigan; Northwestern National Life Insurance Co., Minneapolis, Minnesota; Irene Kaastrup–Olsen of George Jensen, New York; Phoenix Mutual Life Insurance Co., Hartford, Connecticut; Poster Originals, Limited, New York City; Binney and Smith, Co.; Roberto Rendueles, Chief, Office of Public Information, World Health Organization; Alfred Charles Stern of Schainen Stern Design Associates, Inc., New York; Thorne, Architect; Marion L. Vanderbilt of Skidmore, Owings, and Merrill, New York; June R. Vollman of United States Plywood Corporation; George D. Wintress of The Seamen's Bank for Savings, New York.

Acknowledgments

I wish to express my sincere thanks to the many art educators throughout the United States for providing me with the outstanding examples of student work to illustrate various chapters of this book: Nelson Adlin, Art Department, Baltimore Junior College, Maryland; Rosemary Beymer, Kansas City Public Schools, Kansas City, Missouri; Wilma Bradbury, Public Schools, Falmouth Foreside, Maine; Gerald F. Brommer, Lutheran High School, Los Angeles, California; Frederick Gill, Philadelphia Public Schools, Pennsylvania; Robert Goldman, Philadelphia Public Schools, Pennsylvania; Al Hurwitz, Dade County Public Schools, Miami, Florida; Ivan Johnson, Florida State University, Tallahassee, Florida; Jo Kowalchuk, Dade County Public Schools, Miami, Florida; Julian Levy, Philadelphia Public Schools, Pennsylvania; Leon Mead, Head, University School Art Program, F.S.U., Tallahassee, Florida; Richard Micherdzinski, Baltimore City Public Schools, Baltimore, Maryland; John C. Nerreau, Public Schools, Bridgeport, Connecticut; Sarita Rainey, Public Schools, Montclair, New Jersey; Clyde Roberts, Washington County Public Schools, Maryland; Olive Roberts, Vancouver Public Schools, Vancouver, Washington; Marion Senechal, Scotia-Glenville Central Schools, New York; Richard Summers, Frederick County Public Schools, Maryland; Mary Beth Wackwitz, Prince George's County, Maryland; Mary Wellham, Anne Arundel County Public Schools, Maryland.